Upgrade to Free:

The Best Free & Low-Cost Online Tools & Apps

Beth Ziesenis

Publishing

Acknowledgements

It takes more than an unlimited supply of cupcakes and a wardrobe of comfy sweat-pants to write a data-rich book like this. I'm very fortunate to have had the support of scores of friends, family members and professional colleagues as I collected and sorted hundreds of free and low-cost tech tools.

One of the biggest thanks goes to D.J. Rausa, my husband and best friend. Through-out the writing process, D.J. swore to me that the sweatpants looked sexy and the cupcakes were justified. He put up with the frantic writing pace and didn't seem to mind when his innocent, "Good morning, sunshine," was met with "Oh my God! I don't have time for that! Can't you see I'm writing a book?" I don't think I could have paid anyone to be as supportive as he was.

Speaking of paying someone for support, I couldn't have done this project without my assistant, Claire Rose Parrish. She spent hours surfing the web on my laptop and entering details about tools into a database, seated somewhat awkwardly on a chair I stole from the conference room. Claire helped me manage the scope of the project by threatening to cut off my cupcake supply if I added more tools to the list. I'm forever grateful that she took time out of her studies to work with me.

I also want to thank the incredibly supportive runners and cyclists from the Leuke-mia and Lymphoma Society's Team in Training community here in San Diego. I've been running marathons with these folks for four years, and they've kept me run-ning and writing as I worked on this book.

Finally, a huge thanks to my family in the Denver area. To my sister, Sarah, for always answering the phone when I needed it most. To Papa, who brilliantly knew when to say, "Sounds like you're upset. Let me get your mother on the phone." And to Mom, who decided I should be a writer when I was two.

4

If you bought this book,
chances are you spend too much time on your computer.

This book is dedicated to you,
with hopes that you'll discover free and low-cost tools to increase
your efficiency and make your computer time more productive.

And then you can take the free time you've discovered and the
money you've saved and step out for a cupcake.

We could all use more cupcakes.

CONT

ENTS

7

8

9

In Lieu of an Intro:

Top 10 (Actually 12) Questions You Should Ask Before Reading

Here's a short list of frequently asked questions about why this book exists and what to expect.

❶ WHY'D YOU WRITE THE BOOK?

I was a member of the American Society of Association Executives, now ASAE & The Center for Association Leadership. We have an active forum of association executives, and I posted this question in the summer of 2007:

What are your favorite free and low-cost tech tools? *These are the ones you discover late one night when you're still in the office – the ones you are excited to install and share with your colleagues with an immediate "Hey – look what I found!" e-mail.*

Within two days I had a list of 60+ tools. Everyone loved sending in their favorite discoveries. I put them together into a list and distributed it to the forum. People started requesting the list for their newsletters and magazines and more tools kept coming in. Finally I created a home for all of them at www.AskBethZ.com.

Last year, publisher Mark Long from TSTC Publishing in Waco wrote me a note. "Have you ever thought about turning your tools into a book?" Five months later, I submitted the manuscript to his team to work their magic.

❷ WON'T THE TOOLS IN THIS BOOK BE OUTDATED AS SOON AS IT'S WRITTEN?

The changes in technology make my head spin. Each day, heck ... each hour, I hear about cool and cooler things that will make my life easier, keep me more organized and give me more access to resources. Thus, I'm sure that in the time it takes you to read this answer, a half dozen new tools are appearing on the market.

But looking back at my original list of 60+ tools from 2007, perhaps three of those are no longer around. In fact, many of those veterans are in this book. When picking tools to include in the book, I looked at their history, their funding, their plans and more. More than 100 of the companies filled out my survey asking for information, and I take that as a more serious commitment to their longevity. Thus, I have confidence that the tools in this book are built to last through 2011 and beyond.

③ I'M NOT A COMPUTER GADGET GEEK, AND SOMETIMES I DON'T EVEN LIKE COMPUTERS. WHY SHOULD I READ THIS BOOK?

I wrote this book for computer users just like you – ordinary, everyday professionals and students who spend hours every week in front of the computer, whether they like it or not. The tools in this book are tools I use to make my life easier. If I didn't understand a tool or couldn't imagine that I would ever have a need for it, I left it out (with a couple of exceptions of deals that looked so good I couldn't help but share).

③ₐ I AM A GADGET GEEK, AND I LOVE COMPUTERS. WHY SHOULD I READ THIS BOOK?

Every time I run into someone who knows more about computers than I do (and there are plenty), I'm able to introduce them to a new tool they didn't know existed. Experienced computer users will find treasures here, too, and I invite them to send even more of their favorite tools to me at beth@askbethz.com.

④ WHY DO THESE PEOPLE CREATE FREE TOOLS ANYWAY?

I consider myself more of a computer enthusiast than a full-fledged computer geek. Thus, I've never been involved in software development, wouldn't know how to write a line of code if my life depended on it and in general happily use the free tools without really worrying about how they came to be. That being said, I have noticed that free and low-cost tools tend to fall into four categories of reasons behind their development:

➡ OPEN SOURCE COMMUNITIES

The open source movement almost a decade ago had communities of coders and software developers coming together to share ideas and collaborate on code. People have written entire books on the rise of this movement, which popularized such terms as "donationware," "freeware" and "shareware."

The communities that develop these tools have a passion for open source sharing, and they generally volunteer their time to improving their products. SourceForge (page 145) is a notable example of this type of community, and it has given rise to Audacity (page 91), one of my favorites.

➡ TALENTED INDEPENDENT CODERS

Frequently I run across really smart guys who create a cool, quirky tool just because they see a need and have some time. It's a challenge for them, and they create something to share with friends and family, and eventually it catches on.

I worry a little about the longevity of these tools because they depend on the volunteer time from a single developer. They tend to be updated less often and sometimes fall behind in terms of compatibility with updated platforms. But the cool thing is that some of them are more or less evergreen, like 10 Minute Mail (page 173). In 2006 a cool guy named Devon Hilliard started this service, which creates a temporary e-mail address that you can use when you don't want to register for something. Devon supports his efforts with ad revenue, and I can't imagine his tool will fade away.

➡ COMPANIES THAT WANT YOU TO BUY THEIR PRODUCTS

Most of the tools in this book fall into this category. Companies frequently create a free version of their tool or service to give you a taste of how wonderful your life will be if you buy their full version. I've found that the free versions work for most of my needs, but I'm happy to upgrade if it's a service I use often, such as Jing (page 66).

In addition, some companies create free tools to give to the world to improve their reputations. For example, Twelpforce (page 163) is Best Buy's free service that allows you to ask a question of their computer experts via Twitter (page 219). Many companies will release their tools for free in beta while they're trying to work out the kinks. Once they stabilize the software, they usually start charging.

➡ BAD GUYS WITH BAD INTENTIONS

Sometimes free is free, and sometimes free comes with all kinds of nasty strings. Some of the free tools you run across may require you to register, and then they sell your name and information to advertisers. Other tools are even worse. When you download their tools or even sometimes just visit their site, they install a virus, a Trojan or other evil object. These tools have sparked a whole new category of vocabulary: "spyware," "malware," "grayware" and "adware." I bet you can guess what vocabulary I use when I refer to these guys.

Obviously I've worked hard to avoid these bad types of tools, but you'll be entering at your own risk. The information provided in this book is given in good faith and is only an indication of what I have discovered in trying out the software and applications detailed herein. You must make your own judgements, and neither I nor TSTC Publishing can accept liability for any damage or injury sustained as a result of trying what we have tried, nor can we accept any liability arising out of incomplete or incorrect information. That said, hey, it's the absolute best good faith effort I can give!

❺ HOW CAN I AVOID THE TOOLS THAT ARE SCAMS?

Here are five ways to guard yourself against the bad guys who offer free tools with hidden agendas:

- ➡ Register with care and use temporary e-mails until you trust

- ➡ Keep your virus software up to date

- ➡ Download your free and low-cost software from trusted clearinghouses such as SourceForge and CNET

- ➡ Search the Web with the name of a new tool

- ➡ Check out their Privacy Statement (although I suppose if they're really bad guys, they will lie about what they're doing with your info)

Throughout the book, you'll notice Privacy Checks to help you get in the habit of reading the fine print.

⑥ HAVE YOU EVER BEEN DUPED BY A BAD GUY?

Uh, yeah. It wasn't pretty. I downloaded a free tool to help monitor my computer time to keep me more productive. The company looked legit and still exists, but it installed strangely and added an obscure, suspicious executable file that I never got rid of. (Read the story "When Bad Apps Happen to Good People," page 170.)

⑦ ARE ALL THESE TOOLS FOR BOTH PC AND MAC? WHAT BROWSERS CAN I USE?

Many of these tools are what they call Software as a Service, or SaaS. This means that they live on the Web, not as a download on your computer. They run in all kinds of browsers and on all kinds of platforms.

Thus, it's safe to say many of these tools will work on Mac and PC and will work in most browsers. Where appropriate, I noted the browser or the platform if it was limited. Since these tools are updated so quickly, you should always check the system requirements before diving in.

⑧ (NAME OF TOOL) IS A FANTASTIC TOOL! WHY DIDN'T YOU INCLUDE IT IN THE BOOK?

I could spend a lifetime (and perhaps I will) seeking out new tools and writing books about them, and I'd still miss some. For this book, I investigated hundreds of tools and tried to share my favorites. Yep, there are plenty more out there. I'll keep documenting them on www.AskBethZ.com.

I welcome new tools from contributors! Please send your discoveries, feedback and success stories to beth@askbethz.com. And please let me know if you discover a bad guy tool – one that installs something nasty on your computer, sends out spam after registration or in general just messes with your life.

⑨ MY SMARTPHONE HAS A MILLION FREE AND LOW-COST APPLICATIONS. WHY DIDN'T YOU INCLUDE THEM?

This book focuses on online computer tools and ones you can download to your personal machines. The smartphone world changes even more quickly than the online world, and any list of great smartphone apps belongs on a website where it can be updated daily. This book should be a great reference tool for 2011 and beyond, without becoming hopelessly outdated.

⑩ I LOVE THE TOOLS IN THIS BOOK, AND I CAN'T WAIT FOR THE 2012 EDITION FOR MORE. WHERE CAN I GET NEW TOOLS NOW?

Each week I update www.AskBethZ.com with the latest tool discoveries. You can sign up to get e-mails when a new tool comes out, or add your name to the newsletter list for a monthly summary of the best new ones. In addition, you'll find the tools from this book on the site, and you can look them up to see any changes in a tool's status.

⑪ SO, BETH, ANOTHER THING: HOW COME SOME OF THE WEB ADDRESSES IN THIS BOOK HAVE "WWW" AT THE BEGINNING OF THEM BUT OTHERS DON'T?

Back in ye olden days of the Internet – you know, about 18 months ago – a "www" at the beginning of all URLs was pretty ubiquitous. However, that's becoming less and less true as time goes on. So, when you see a Web address in this book without one – such as bit.ly on (page 210) – it's not because anything has been left out but, rather, that where you're going just has one of those newfangled addresses.

⑫ BETH, WHAT'S UP WITH THOSE CRAZY BOXES WITH LITTLE BLACK AND WHITE SQUARES IN THEM?

Quick Response (QR) codes can be scanned using a QR reader – there are tons of free ones available – on a smartphone. QR codes can do a variety of things: add contact info, dial a phone number or send a text message. The ones in this book link to the web page for the tool being discussed. For example, if you scan this QR code, it will take you to my Ask Beth Z website. For me, it's a way of making the book more user friendly – who wants to type in all those web address? – while, at the same time, allowing you to get the latest information about each of the tools in the book.

1

Tools for Efficiency at Home and on the Road

Where does the time go, and why does everything I do during the day just seem to take so long?

These are the questions you might ask that lead you to discovering these tools. The first part of the chapter focuses on blocking out distractions and cutting down on external noise so you can make your time at a computer more productive. I use several of these tools each day, including K9 Web Protection (page 19) and Work-Time (page 18). A couple of the tools I've only needed once or twice, such as The Alphabetizer (page 22), but they're essential time-savers when you need them. In addition, I love the tools that help you be more efficient (and green!) when you print.

When you're on the road, it's even harder to be productive and efficient, so the next section looks at tools that simplify your life when you're traveling. LogMeIn (page 24) saves my hide by letting me remote into my desktop computer, and some of the travel-planning tools were submitted by veteran travelers who adore their ability to help you travel more comfortably for less money.

IN THIS CHAPTER:

WorkTime

www.nestersoft.com/worktime

$29.95

*One-time fee
for home edition*

 YOU NEED THIS TOOL, BUT YOU'RE NOT GOING TO LIKE IT

Do you ever look at the clock and say, "What the heck have I done for the last two hours?"

Install WorkTime, and you'll know in an instant. WorkTime tracks every single activity on your computer in six-second increments. It shows you how long you surf the Web, work on a document, spend writing e-mails. I can't imagine a better tool for understanding where your time goes so you can change habits and increase your productivity.

This is not an attractive program, but it works. I've been using it for almost two years, and I can look back to see every moment that I've spent, including searches for nearby cupcake outlets, updates on *American Idol* and research about my ailing stock portfolio. I sure hope no one ever steals my computers. My history is a little humiliating. WorkTime is perfect for those of us who want to increase our productivity, or anyone who has to record hours on a project.

ALSO CHECK OUT

 **Chrometa** (www.chrometa.com) Chrometa has a nice tagging tool that helps you keep track of projects. I also like that if you're gone for a while (out searching for cupcakes, perhaps), a window pops up when you get back to let you record your away time. Pricing starts at $19 a month for three months of data and goes up to $99 per month for unlimited.

 **RescueTime** (www.rescuetime.com): Lite version is "free forever (but kinda wimpy)," and the Pro version starts at $6 a month.

18

K9 Web Protection

www.k9webprotection.com

FREE

*For personal use;
it sells an enterprise version
for businesses.*

 CONTROL YOUR INTERNET USAGE

I'm in love with K9 Web Protection, a free Internet filtering service. Sure, it's made for parents to protect their kids, but as a professional with a bad Web habit, I appreciate its ability to keep me from wasting my precious time. You set sites that you'd like to limit, and you can eliminate entire categories of sites.

I am particularly bad when it comes to reading news articles. I can read article after article and waste an hour or two ... time just slips away. With K9, you can allow access for 15 minutes or a certain period of time. That way you can pop in to check on your friends in Facebook, but soon you're back at work. K9 also watches out for Web threats such as phishing and malware.

ALSO CHECK OUT

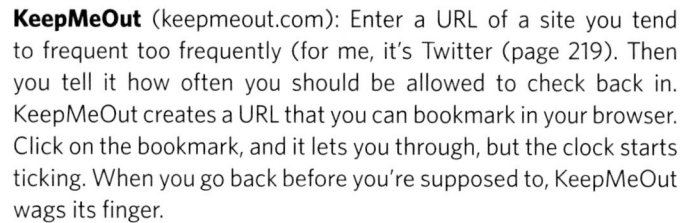

 **KeepMeOut** (keepmeout.com): Enter a URL of a site you tend to frequent too frequently (for me, it's Twitter (page 219). Then you tell it how often you should be allowed to check back in. KeepMeOut creates a URL that you can bookmark in your browser. Click on the bookmark, and it lets you through, but the clock starts ticking. When you go back before you're supposed to, KeepMeOut wags its finger.

 **LeechBlock** (www.proginosko.com/leechblock.html):
A simple Firefox add-on that helps you block sites that suck your productivity. I set it so I limit my Twitter (page 219) time to five minutes every two hours during the workday.

DarkCopy

www.darkcopy.com

FREE

 SIMPLIFY THE WRITING PROCESS

If you're as old as I am, you'll remember the computers of days gone by, where you had a black screen and a blinking green cursor box. You didn't have to check e-mail every 10 minutes because there was no real e-mail as we know it. No Facebook, no Twitter, no nuthin' ... just you and a blank screen.

DarkCopy brings you back to those days with a simple, elegant tool to help you blot out all the intoxicating distractions of 2011. Just visit the site, expand the black screen to full size, and you're transported back to pre-Windows 3.1. There are absolutely no bells or whistles, and that's what makes it great.

ALSO CHECK OUT

 **Dark Room** (they.misled.us/dark-room): My writer friend Moonbean McQueen (moonbeammcqueen.wordpress.com) loves Dark Room. "I don't know why I love this so much, but I do. I find it easy to use, and it does sort of give me the feeling that I'm in my own little writing world. I prefer its simplicity to Word."

NutshellMail	**FREE**
www.nutshellmail.com	

 **CONDENSE YOUR SOCIAL MEDIA UPDATES INTO ONE DIGEST**

Are you overwhelmed with all the separate e-mails you get from Facebook, Twitter (page 219) and that e-mail address you never find time to check?

NutshellMail condenses all the chatter and sends you one snapshot e-mail of your online activity. You can choose how often you get a digest and where it goes. When it arrives, you can respond directly to the actionable items (like responding to your mother's wall post about whether you've had a cupcake lately) through the e-mail without having to log in and check every site.

☑ **PRIVACY CHECK:** NutshellMail promises they'll never rent, sell or use your e-mail or other registration information to send you advertisements. In addition, the system that sends you e-mail is automated, so they pledge they are not reading your e-mails. They keep copies of your social media updates as well as the e-mails they send for a limited time.

21

Readability

readability.com

FREE

 MAKE CLUTTERED WEB PAGES READABLE

CHEAP TIP:
Before you create the bookmarklet, play around with the settings to adjust the margins, choose the size and more.

Bestselling author Dan Pink (www.danpink.com) contributed Readability as his favorite free tool. "It's a nifty little bookmarklet I've added to my browser that, with one click, strips away the ads and nonsense on any web page and displays just the text in large type running down the center of the page. It makes reading articles on the web – something I do way too much of – much, much easier."

My running buddy Erik Staley, principal consultant for FDA compliance and validation firm Valicom (www.valicom.com), also loves Readability. "Somewhere deep in a sea of banner ads and flash graphics is the reason that I went to a Web page in the first place," Erik said. "Readability strips out the nonsense and formats the main text into something that's, well, readable. Plus I can use it in conjunction with PDF Annotator or Word to take notes on top of the cleaned-up page."

Just drag the Readiblity bookmarklet to your browser, and click it when you want to render a Web page more readable. Poof ... all the ads and other nonsense slip away, and you're left with black words on a white screen – infinitely easier to read.

22

JUST 'CUZ YOU CAN

 How nifty! **The Alphabetizer** (alphabetizer.flap.tv) will alphabetize, randomize or reverse any list you need handled. Just cut and paste your list into the box and choose the options you want (Ignore Indefinite Articles, Remove Duplicates, etc). When the page refreshes, you've got the list you want! Couldn't be easier.

Travel Tools

Several of my regular readers are super travelers, and they've contributed a few essential low-cost or free tools that they use to help them sit up (in first class) and fly right.

 **ExpertFlyer** (www.expertflyer.com): ExpertFlyer can help you find the best deals, sneak into first-class opportunities and maximize your upgrades. A little pricy at $4.99 a month for basic level or $9.99 a month for the premium version, but heavy-duty travelers will save more than that in a couple of flights.

 **Seatguru** (www.seatguru.com): Seatguru helps you pick the best spot on the plane when you're booking your ticket. You get detailed seat maps plus advice about seats with limited recline, reduced legroom and misaligned windows. Check out the color-coding feature to find the best seats, power port locations and more. Free.

 **TripIt** (www.tripit.com): Pull all of your travel plans together in one spot to build an intinerary, get organized and keep track of everything you need for your travels. DrGreene.com's Cheryl Greene declared this site, "So valuable for travel planning." TripIt is free, and the Pro version is $49 a year with extra features such as keeping track of your frequent flyer miles.

ALSO CHECK OUT

 **Kuku Klok** (www.kukuklok.com): Are you one of those people who likes to set two or three alarms when you travel because one of them may not work? Use set Kuku Klok on your laptop for a little extra assurance.

 **NakedAlarmClock.com** (www.nakedalarmclock.com): It does the same thing as Kuku Klok, but I love a tool with the word "Naked" in it.

23

LogMeIn

www.logmein.com

FREE

 A FREE (AND RELIABLE) REMOTE DESKTOP TOOL

I regularly remote into my office computer when I'm traveling so WorkTime (page 18) will track my time. For a while, I used Windows Live Mesh (page 151), but the software got to where it wasn't playing well with the other applications. So I returned to the award-winning LogMeIn, which I had abandoned because the free version didn't have all the cool features that Live Mesh does, most notably the ability to drag and drop files across the computers.

But LogMeIn Free has made some improvements, and it's now my favorite again. Now LogMeIn allows me to copy something on one computer and paste it to the other, so I can copy a whole file to transfer. Plus, I use multiple monitors on my desktop, and LogMeIn lets me switch between them with the click of a button. The biggest thing I like about it is that it works, and, of course, it's free. The professional version is quite reasonably priced as well ($70 a year for one computer), plus they have other services such as backup.

Their $29.99 iPhone app is phenomenal. Push your iPhone or iPad screen a couple of times, and within seconds you're seeing and controlling your remote computer. Well worth the money.

ALSO CHECK OUT

 **GoToMyPC** (www.gotomypc.com): Features are very comparable to LogMeIn Pro, and the company is one I trust. Free 30-day trial, then starting at $9.95 a month. The GoToMyPC app for iPhone and iPad is free with your subscription.

Print Friendly	**FREE**
www.PrintFriendly.com	

 MAKE A PRINT-FRIENDLY VERSION OF ANY WEB PAGE

I love things that make you more productive and help the environment. Print Friendly takes any Web page and reformats it for printing, making sure you don't waste pages when the text runs off the page. If you remove all the stuff you don't need from a 10-page document and end up with a 3-pager, you save $.70 and all that paper!

You can also easily remove pictures for printing or save as a PDF. Another cool feature is that anyone can add a little widget to a blog or site to allow readers to make the page print friendly.

Melinda Urick, copywriter and social media networker (melindaurick.com), says, "Print Friendly is fantastic. I don't own a printer (and don't particularly like the waste of paper) and bookmarks never worked well for me. Seeing a PDF on my desktop (and organized in a folder) increases my sanity!

JUST 'CUZ YOU CAN

 **Printer.com**, a company that rates printers by price and efficiency, studied ink usage in printed fonts and determined that switching from good old Arial font to Century Gothic or Times New Roman will save the average user about $20 a year on ink. Other economical fonts are Calibri, Verdana, Arial and Sans Serif.

 **GreenPrint Software** (www.printgreener.com): Download the software to install GreenPrint options as printer drivers. When you print, you see a preview of the document, and you can cut out unnecessary graphics, skip over pages with just one line of text and more. Also lets you print to a PDF. Free for personal use on Windows machines. One-time fee of $19 for a few more features and Mac capability.

PrinterShare

www.printeranywhere.com

FREE

 PRINT TO ANY LOCAL COMPUTER

Reading about how PrinterShare works kind of makes my eyes cross, but here's the bottom line: once you download the software and set it up, you can be in someone else's office and print to the local computer without having to break out the thumb drive. You can even send documents on certain smartphones to the printer. Smart idea, and it keeps you from having to walk around pathetically with a thumb drive asking people to print something out for you when you're on the road.

SMARTPHONE APPS: iPhone and Android

ALSO CHECK OUT

 **Xerox Mobile Express Driver** (bit.ly/U2Fmobileexpressdriver): Print to any printer when you log into a network.

2

Personal Organization Tools

It's hard enough to put your ducks in a row. Where in the world do you store them?

This section focuses on tools that help you get organized. From Evernote (page 28), the ultimate notetaking tool, to Mint.com (page 33), an online financial manager, these resources help you manage your physical, financial and online "stuff" that clutters your computer, your desk and your brain.

IN THIS CHAPTER:

Evernote

www.evernote.com

FREE

Or a Premium level for $5 per month or $45 a year.

 THE GRANDDADDY OF NOTETAKING

Evernote gives you the ability to take notes and capture ideas no matter where you are on your computer. As soon as you install it, you have little icons here and there that allow you to throw Web pages, documents, pictures, ideas, screenshots and anything else into your organization center.

Evernote integrates with all kinds of other free and low-cost tools in this book, including Pelotonics (page 125) and TimeBridge (page 48). It competes directly with Microsoft's OneNote, which costs about $80 bucks if you buy it alone.

SMARTPHONE APPS:

➡ BlackBerry

➡ iPhone

➡ Android

➡ Palm Pre

Xobni

www.xobni.com/lp/CF

 ORGANIZE YOUR OUTLOOK INBOX

According to the company, Bill Gates called Xobni "the next generation of social networking."

Xobni is "inbox" in reverse, but this free Outlook gadget is anything but backward. Once you install Xobni, your Xobni dashboard appears in your inbox. When you get an e-mail, you see all kinds of fun facts, such as the e-mail conversations you've exchanged, the times of the day that your contact usually sends e-mails and the other people who have been included in your conversation. Plus all the attachments you've exchanged are listed together.

There are plenty of other little tricks, but my favorite feature is a simple one. How many times have you gotten an e-mail about a meeting and had to switch to your calendar to check availability? You have to switch back and forth between the inbox and the calendar, cutting and pasting phone numbers, figuring out meeting times, etc. But when you switch to the calendar, Xobni keeps the last e-mail you viewed in the dashboard. No more flipping back and forth.

SMARTPHONE APPS: BlackBerry

MyStickies

FREE

www.mystickies.com

 ADD NOTES TO YOUR WORLD, WEB AND ALL

MyStickies is a bookmarking system that allows you to place little yellow squares of digital paper, sticky notes, if you will, anywhere you visit on the Web. You can browse, search, sort and edit your stickies from any computer with Internet access.

When you find a page you like, MyStickies lets you mark the page to help you remember why you liked it. Look for MyStickies to add multilingual notes, browser extensions for Internet Explorer and Safari, sharing tags' notes and individual notes with friends, rich text notes (bold, italics and links) and more.

ALSO CHECK OUT

 **Google Reader** (bit.ly/U2Fgoogreader): Kendra Kellog of the E-Advocate Network (cool concept: "Tech for change, design for humanity," e-advocate.org) says of Google Reader, "What's old is new again!" because of some of its advanced capabilities. Google Reader lets you add a button to your browser to "Note in Reader," allowing you to add critical information to Reader with your comment. From Reader you can send targeted, relevant information to your individual social media profiles. She uses it as a social media dashboard. "It works perfectly during newsworthy events, crisis or campaigns when rapid, targeted sharing is critical."

 **Instapaper** (www.instapaper.com): Gini Dietrich of the marketing firm Arment Dietrich (armentdietrich.com) loves Instapaper for saving the articles she runs across online. "I used to solely use it online, but now I have it on my iPhone and it's FANTASTIC for down time (cabs, in line, etc.) to catch up on my reading."

JUST 'CUZ YOU CAN

 There's nothing flashy about **Printable Rulers** (www.vendian.org/mncharity/dir3/paper_rulers). I have no idea if it'll ever be updated. It is what it is, and I like what it is: templates for disposable paper rulers when you need them. Take their advice and print the ruler on an overhead transparency or on cardstock to make your new ruler a little more sturdy. Free.

Know Your Stuff

FREE

www.knowyourstuff.org

 KEEP YOUR HOME INVENTORY ONLINE

Walk through the Know Your Stuff Home Inventory wizard to capture everything you need to know about yourself, your location and your insurance company should you need to make a claim from your insurance.

The information is stored online, so even if your computer is compromised, you can easily provide the right information to your insurance company should a disaster strike or a burglary occur.

ALSO CHECK OUT

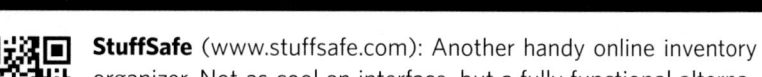

StuffSafe (www.stuffsafe.com): Another handy online inventory organizer. Not as cool an interface, but a fully functional alternative.

Mint.com	**FREE**
www.mint.com	

 FREE ONLINE MONEY MANAGER

Gather all your financial information into one area, then set up an account on Mint.com to start tracking your expenses and managing your budget. The system takes you a few minutes to set up, and then all of your expenses and income are in the same place.

Mint makes its money by providing recommendations that could save you money ... a suggestion of a credit card that has a lower interest rate, a recommendation of a high-interest bearing savings account, etc. If you take them up on their offer, Mint makes money. If not, you can still use their budgeting system for free.

Mint.com has won awards from Kiplinger.com, *Time*, *Money*, *PCWorld* and life-hacker. Everybody loves it. It's secure, easy to use and just makes sense. And the website looks cool, too.

Originally, the name of the company was Money Intelligence, but they changed it to Mint. In 2010 it won the SXSW Web Award in the Classics category, which is kind of funny since to me a birth year of 2005 doesn't make it that much of a classic.

According to the staff, the typical Mint.com user finds $1,000 in savings in the first visit. Mint.com's IRA center can help people save up to $1,500 annually on their taxes by instructing them if a traditional or Roth IRA is best for them and then recommending companies through which they can open one.

SMARTPHONE APPS: iPhone and Android

ALSO CHECK OUT

 **Wesabe** (www.wesabe.com): Part money management tool, part community. Organize your finances online, and use the wisdom of the people in the community to help you find solutions to your money challenges by interacting with the community. Free.

33

MAPMYself

www.mapul.com

 FREE ONLINE MIND-MAPPING SOFTWARE

I'm a linear chick myself, and I actually enjoy making outlines, writing lists and thinking of things in a step-by-step process. But whole generations of people were introduced to the concept of mind mapping for brainstorming. Instead of making a list, mind-mapping systems ask you to create bubbles of information and connect them to other bubbles of information.

MAPMYself (aka Mapul) has cool graphics and a nicely functional free version that allows you to create and share your own mind maps.

ALSO CHECK OUT

 **Wridea** (www.wridea.com): A pretty linear approach to brainstorming as opposed to idea webs or bubbles or whatever they call them, and the Idea Rain feature lets you contemplate your ideas as they flow down the page. You can also share your ideas with others in a flash. Free.

3

E-mail Blast Services and Surveys

Are you guilty of using the BCC field to send out e-mails to your colleagues, customers or other contacts?

Folks, there's a better way, and the government would prefer (might insist) that you change your process.

Using an e-mail service is a smart idea for so many reasons. First of all, the automated services out there help you to adhere to the basic rules of the CAN-SPAM Act, which established regulations about e-mails that contain advertisements. In a nutshell, the act says you have to make it clear that your e-mail is an advertisement, include your physical address and make it very easy for someone to opt out of receiving your e-mails.

Secondly, if you're doing any type of marketing with e-mails, you need to know what works and what doesn't. E-mail blast companies will help you track the efficiency of your e-mails – how many people opened them and how many people actually clicked on something once they were opened. These are important statistics to help guide your campaigns.

And thirdly, using a service looks better to your contacts. When I get an e-mail that says from John Smith to John Smith, I know that John Smith sent this to a billion people in the BCC field, and it diminishes my interest in his message. E-mail services can help you personalize your messages so John Smith can send a "Dear Beth" note to just me.

This section also covers surveys and other ways to seek feedback from your network and community. These tools are essential, professional and just plain smart for gathering and organizing information and engaging the people in your networks.

IN THIS CHAPTER:

MailChimp
www.mailchimp.com

FREE
Up to 2,000 subscribers and 12,000 emails a month.

 THE E-MAIL SERVICE WITH THE CUTE MONKEY

Way back when I was searching for a low-cost e-mail service, I have to admit I was turned off by the MailChimp monkey. Sure, it's cute. But I didn't want cute. I wanted something professional. So I passed MailChimp by to choose Constant Contact (page 38).

But I've reconsidered my decision, and as soon as I can come up for air, I think I'll be switching to MailChimp. Both services offer the basics: e-mail templates, tracking, list management, etc. But MailChimp makes it easier for me to test two different subject lines to see which one people are more likely to open. As they say on their website, MailChimp has "more e-mail marketing tools than you can shake a banana at." Yeah, it's corny. But I'm willing to switch to corny for more capabilities.

In addition, MailChimp integrates some of my other favorite free tools into their system, so I can search iStockphoto (page 81) for the perfect graphic, add a border to it in Picnik (page 54) and throw a little widget onto my WordPress sites (page 110) to encourage people to sign up.

"The WordPress plug-in that goes with it is really great, as you get to see correlation between marketing campaigns and website traffic."

Julie Mazziotta, Web designer and marketing consultant.
www.juliemazziotta.com.

37

Constant Contact

www.constantcontact.com

$15

$15 a month for up to 500 subscribers, then $30 a month for up to 2,500, etc.

 MY FIRST LOVE IN BARGAIN E-MAIL SERVICES

I've encouraged many of my clients to sign up for Constant Contact. They have a wide variety of templates that make my life easier, and their tracking is robust and reliable. What's more, I love their tips and newsletters, all designed to help you do a better job of standing out in people's e-mail boxes.

One of the reasons that I fell in love with Constant Contact was because they offer free live courses all over the country. I attended a half-day course on e-mail basics, and I still use some of the examples they gave us in the course when I teach others about e-mails.

They've been around since 1998 (another plus), and they've done some wonderful things to earn the wonderful reputation they enjoy.

JUST 'CUZ YOU CAN

 **Earth Class Mail** (www.earthclassmail.com) is what they call "digital mail management." You use their service to get a real address at one of a number of places across the United States. When your mail arrives, Earth Class Mail scans the envelope and lets you decide if you want to recycle it or pay a small fee to have it scanned or forwarded to you in hard copy. They'll even deposit your checks for you – starting between $20 and $40 a month, depending on the volume. I definitely see this as an essential tool that's worth the price if you are a frequent traveler who receives mail you can't afford to wait to receive.

Wufoo

wufoo.com

FREE

For 3 forms, and other levels start at $14.95 a month.

CREATE ONLINE FORMS, SURVEYS AND INVITES

You have to give a second look to a company that named itself after the musical groups Wu-Tang Clan and the Foo Fighters. Wufoo helps you create contact forms, online surveys and invitations so you can collect the data, registrations and online payments you need without writing a single line of code.

Wufoo forms can be seemlessly embedded into your website and send collected data to your other favorite services such as MailChimp (page 37) and Basecamp (page 123) in real time. The Wufoo folks tell me they're looking to add more integrations, payment processors and more.

The reader who contributed it said she uses it for her association for scholarship application forms, speaker forms, award nominations and "other stuff that our website hosting/design folks would charge big bucks for," and added, "I LOVE the e-mail feature as I e-mail submissions for scholarships and award nominations to my committee members."

39

ALSO CHECK OUT

Formstack (www.formstack.com): Same basic pricing structure as Wufoo, and nonprofits get a 10 percent discount. Formstack also has an iPhone app.

JUST 'CUZ YOU CAN

 With e-mail, social networks and other ways to communicate, our names (and sometimes pictures) are always on our posts and comments. And sometimes we may hesitate to say exactly what's on our minds in a public forum. **Quetzi** (www.quetzi.com) is a free service that allows you to set up a question thread to seek anonymous feedback for any question. You can invite people to contribute, and you can even allow your invitees to invite others.

 Need more help from friends and experts? You might try **Bulbstorm** (www.bulbstorm.com), an online community where you upload your ideas for a great marketing campaign, innovative company and more, and others (invited by you) chime in with feedback.

SurveyMonkey

www.surveymonkey.com

FREE

Free for the basics and $24.99 for all the features.

 CHEAP AND EASY WEB SURVEYS

No less than three readers recommended SurveyMonkey as "worth the money." SurveyMonkey lets you design surveys easily using more than a dozen question types. I've created simple forms for feedback from my clients as well as elaborate surveys with custom skip logic, graphics and customized filters. The free version gives you 100 responses per survey and up to 15 questions. But, as the readers pointed out, for just $16.99 a month you get a whole host of other useful features. Being able to customize surveys with skip logic is well worth the cost.

As the SurveyMonkey people told me, "Chances are you know someone who is hooked on the monkey." They claim that all of the Fortune 100 companies use their service, as well as other businesses, academic institutions and organizations of all shapes and sizes.

CHEAP TIP

Sure, you only get 15 questions on a free survey, but you can add questions that have multiple text boxes and answer options to solicit a lot more information. For example, customize SurveyMonkey's demographic question to collect a whole host of data fields that all count as one of your 15 questions.

ALSO CHECK OUT

 **Zoomerang** (www.zoomerang.com): Free for 12 questions and up to 100 responses. I have commitment issues, so I didn't want to commit to their $199 yearly fee, but the pricing ends up working out to be about the same as SurveyMonkey. Nonprofits and academic groups pay just $149.

CHEAP CASE STUDY	**Use surveys to collect data for newsletters, books and other compilations**
	Beth Ziesenis

Many of my clients create organization newsletters, and I customize surveys to help them collect information from their various departments. Instead of the coordinator having to cut and paste info received via e-mail from six department heads, everyone uses a link to fill out the survey each month, and I simply download and format the responses.

In addition, I used SurveyMonkey to collect the data for this book. Readers, vendors and my assistant entered information about their favorite free and low-cost tech tools into a survey, and I downloaded and sorted the data into chapters, with the help of the mail merge feature in Microsoft Word.

42

Wikispaces

www.wikispaces.com

 GOT WIKI?

Sometimes you need to call upon a whole community to collaborate. Wikispaces lets you create an online library of information that you and your peers can populate. The content is long-lived, regularly updated and built by your peers. You can set it up so that guests can edit pages without an account, and it can be written in any language. Wikispaces handles the hosting and the backups, so all you need to do is set it up and invite people.

More features and an ad-free interface start at $50 a year, and using your own domain will cost about $200 a year. Schools and institutions can have what they call Private Label wikis starting at $1,000 a year.

43

4
Meeting Planning Tools

Does this look like any string of e-mails you've received when you're trying to schedule a meeting?

Me: "Ok, so the meeting is scheduled for Tuesday at noon. Does everyone have the call-in number?"

Attendee 1: "Oh, you said Tuesday. I can't make Tuesday. How about Wednesday at 3?"

Attendee 2: "I can't make Wednesday. How about the following Monday?"

Attendee 3: "Wait, which time zone? What day?"

Attendee 4: [Silence]

Attendee 5: "What meeting?"

Luckily several people have turned me on to free meeting planning tools that help busy people coordinate schedules. This section profiles some of my favorite free and low-cost meeting schedulers and event-planning tools to allow you to bring everyone together without spending a month trying to find a date, time and system that works for everyone.

IN THIS CHAPTER:

Doodle

www.doodle.com

 EASY MEETING SCHEDULING WITH NO REGISTRATION

The last thing you want to do when you're trying to get head honchos to meet with you is to make them register to be able to choose a good time to meet.

Doodle is cool. Without ever entering your e-mail address or any personal information, you can set up a grid of possible dates and times for meetings. They generate a link for both your admin view and the participants' responses. Just send them out, and you'll be able to quickly pick a date and time that works for everyone. If you create an account, you have more tracking and other features at your disposal, but it's cool that your participants never have to register if they don't want to.

Doodle also allows you to take a quick poll. It's available in 30 languages, takes time zones into account and has applications for smartphones. Plus users who register can connect Doodle with their own calendars, including Outlook, Google Calendar (page 139), iCal, etc. I like that users can choose three options: Yes, No or If Necessary. That way you end up having a better idea of what will work.

Doodle tells me they came up with a name during a brainstorming session: "it is short, likeable and easy to remember." Founder Myke Naef started Doodle in 2003 when he was trying to find a day for a dinner party.

To get rid of the ads and add other features, upgrade to Premium Doodle for individuals ($29 a year) or Branded Doodle for larger organizations (starting at $119 a year).

SMARTPHONE APPS: iPhone

Doodle is a favorite among students and professionals alike:

"It is easy and efficient: all the time slots are open, and all I have to do is fill them in with my name. A community service organization that I am in, ICARES, uses Doodle to allow people to sign up to table, bake, sell and any other component of the current service project."

Courtney Moltzen, cognitive science major
at the University of California, San Diego

"Doodle works for scheduling busy grad students who can't keep their heads on straight! It's crazy easy to use."

Erin Legacki, Ph.D. candidate in reproductive biology
at the University of California, Davis

"Everyone can post available times on one site. Visual helps identify good meeting times. We use it for scheduling all kinds of phone meetings."

Donna Dunn, national executive director for the Association of
YMCA Professionals, www.aypymca.org

ALSO CHECK OUT

 **Meet with Approval** (www.meetwithapproval.com): Free scheduling for three meetings, but you have to register (invitees don't). The paid level is $30 a year for unlimited meetings and your own branding.

 **MeetingWizard** (www.meetingwizard.com): Started in 2001, MeetingWizard claims it's the first of its kind. 100 percent free. You have to register, but other users don't. I like that you can let others see the other responses and attendees, and you can choose what kind of meeting it is: face-to-face, teleconference, online chat, etc.

 **WhichDateWorks.com** (www.whichdateworks.com): Simple, easy interface with no registration required of anyone. They promise it will be free forever.

TimeBridge

www.timebridge.com

MEETING SCHEDULING PLUS, PLUS, PLUS

TimeBridge has the basic functions of Doodle and the like, but the extra features go further:

➡ Outlook and other calendar tools that install connectors to your schedule on TimeBridge.

➡ Integration with Evernote (page 28) for notetaking, Box.net (page 151) for file sharing and Google Maps for directions.

➡ A meeting room to add notes, create an agenda, communicate quickly with attendees and generally keep yourself organized for the meeting.

➡ Create a group that shows everyone's availability when you schedule regular meetings.

➡ Free conference call numbers and online Web conferencing (see more, page 185) for upgraded levels.

➡ Text message reminders for upgraded levels.

As their site says, "Think of us as your calendar-wrangling, agenda-making, note-taking, team-motivating, secret weapon in the battle against workplace inefficiency. In short, we exist so that you can be a meeting hero!"

SMARTPHONE APPS: iPhone

48

Moreganize

www.moreganize.com

FREE

 ANOTHER MULTITASKING MEETING TOOL

I like the tools that combine different features into one system. Moreganize started out as a student initiative from two law students at the University of Zurich. You can propose meeting times to schedule an event, create polls (anonymous or not) and share to-do lists.

The site looks professional, and the interface is clean and smart. No one has to register, and, for whatever reason, they don't have any plans to create paid versions. In sum, it's no obligation and no cost.

49

Eventbrite

www.eventbrite.com

FREE

For free events, and a small percentage of every ticket sold for paid ones. If you don't sell any tickets, you don't pay anything.

 CREATE AN EVENT AND SELL TICKETS

Groups like Eventbrite know how to help you set up a Web page and promote an event. They charge a small fee (well, small is relative, of course), and they will issue tickets online, process payments, keep track of attendee list and help you organize your marketing.

The awesome thing about Eventbrite is that if your event is free, you can set up to market the event and process tickets for no charge. They also have tips to help you collect donations, and you can connect your event to Facebook and other social networking sites.

ALSO CHECK OUT

 **Guestlist** (www.guestlistapp.com): Like Eventbrite, Guestlist charges nothing if your event costs nothing. They take 2% out of ticket prices for regular events, and charity events are 100% free, no matter how much you charge.

50

5

Picture Editing from Easy to Everything Else

Doesn't everyone needs a few skills to make a cell phone snapshot look clean and professional?

We need to crop out the edge of our thumbs, add captions, resize and add drop shadows. Most of us have a basic, free graphic editor that came with our computer, but if you've ever tried to erase an ex out of a family portrait pixel by pixel using the PC accessory Paint, you know you need more.

This chapter covers tools that range from a 30-second resizer to a sophisticated 3D image creator. In addition, take a look at several free and low-cost picture-editing suites that mimic some of the most popular graphics editors around.

IN THIS CHAPTER:

Cut My Pic

www.cutmypic.com

FREE

 SIZE A GRAPHIC AND ADD ROUNDED CORNERS AND A SHADOW

Simple and easy, Cut My Pic allows users to upload a picture, crop it, add rounded corners and drop in a drop shadow. Truthfully, that's all I need to do on many of the graphics I need to modify.

A few words from Cut My Pic's Sean Crownover:

"We built this tool with simplicity in mind. That is why we made the process into three easy steps that require the least amount time and thought process. Ultimately, we wanted our mothers to be able to use it without explanation! We simply created it to help build our small company's portfolio and show potential customers that we are capable of creating online technologies in a clean, easy-to-use and unobtrusive way."

ALSO CHECK OUT

 **Quick Thumbnail** (www.quickthumbnail.com): Upload a graphic or point to a URL for very, very easy resizing. You can resize with standard dimensions for avatars, icons, etc, but watch out – it'll distort if it's not the same dimensions. You can also apply color filters, a watermark and more good stuff. And, of course, it's free.

53

Picnik

www.picnik.com

EASY ONLINE GRAPHIC EDITING

Picnik is one of those tools that you kind of have to pinch yourself when you find it and ask, "Can this really be free?

If you're like me and completely and utterly confused by Photoshop (what the heck is a "lasso" tool anyway, cowboy?), you need a simple solution to make small changes to pictures. Picnik is the handiest thing I've seen for quick edits to digital pictures. You simply upload an electronic picture (no registration required), and crop it, scale it, create a border, add some text, sprinkle a few hearts for Valentine's Day – whatever you need. Then you download the new file onto your computer.

One of my favorite uses is to help scale pictures. Sometimes low-res graphics lose definition when you grow or shrink them. Picnik helps even out the size without losing resolution. Picnik integrates with many online photo accounts, such as Flickr (page 81) and Picasa (page 82), and plug-ins in Firefox and Chrome make it easier to edit online photos.

Picnik has been around since 2007, and they've won a ton of awards, from *Time Magazine's* 50 Best websites of 2008 to a *Macworld* "Eddy" Award. These people get my money with the upgrade for being so awesome.

Steve Woodruff, social media expert for Impactiviti (www.stevewoodruff.com) says, "Picnik is very simple to use, and quite flexible. I use it to edit or tweak the majority of pictures I use in my blogs."

54

FotoFlexer

www.fotoflexer.com

FREE

 AN EASY GRAPHICS EDITOR WITH
SOPHISTICATED EXTRAS

FotoFlexer is a nice transition tool from the first-grade graphics level of Picnik (page 54) to the graduate-school complexity of the Photoshop replacements like GIMP (page 56). Upload a photo to get started, and you can edit graphics much like Picnik and others: crop, resize, add text, etc.

But FotoFlexer has a few special extras, like the ability to cut out a part of a picture or recolor one section. I also like that you can layer one photo on another, and it has a silly feature that lets you insert a face onto a $100 bill or Paris Hilton's body (let's hope that option quietly slips away). The effects may make you look like a Photoshop pro, but the interface is actually very simple and easy to understand.

55

GIMP

www.gimp.org

FREE

 AN INDUSTRY STANDARD IN THE FREE
GRAPHICS SOFTWARE CATEGORY

GIMP's unfortunate name comes from its humble beginnings as a student project at Berkeley in the mid-1990s. Two guys worked together to create the General Image Manipulation Program, which attracted a loyal following and passionate coders who kept it going. Today the GIMP community still works together to upgrade the program release new versions and get the word out.

Download GIMP to manipulate photos with its many plug-ins and extensions, and visit the forums for lively and informative conversations about tips, bug fixes and more.

56

Paint.net

www.getpaint.net

FREE

 GRAPHICS EDITING SOFTWARE FOR WINDOWS

Beth Camero describes herself as a "she-geek with sci-fi leanings and an unflagging curiosity about everything." She submitted Paint.net, her favorite graphics editing software.

Like GIMP (page 56), Paint.net started out as a college project and has been around for years. Consider it an upgrade from the Paint application that comes as an accessory on PCs. An active community provides support, tutorials and plug-ins.

Beth says she uses Paint.net for sizing graphics, converting one type of graphic to another and creating banners. It's free and lightweight, easy to use and includes many of the same capabilities as Photoshop.

PLATFORMS: Windows

57

Pixlr Editor & Pixlr Express

FREE

www.pixlr.com

 GIMP ONLINE PLUS A FAST-AND-EASY SIMPLE EDITOR

Pixlr is the online form of GIMP (page 56), with a Flash-based uploader that allows you to edit from any computer without having to have the software. Pixlr Editor has many of the same features as Photoshop, and the Express version is perfect for easy, immediate editing. And now they offer the Pixlr Grabber, a plug-in for Firefox, Chrome and a handy download for the Windows desktop.

58

Aviary www.aviary.com	**FREE**

GRAPHICS AND MULTIMEDIA EDITING EXTRAVAGANZA

Aviary belongs in several categories in this book. Their tools, each named after a different bird, include a photo editor, a vector graphic creator, a color analyzer and a special-effects tool.

The Aviary suite:

- ➡ Phoenix: Image Editor
- ➡ Raven: Vector Editor
- ➡ Myna: Audio Editor
- ➡ Peacock: Effects Editor
- ➡ Falcon: Image Markup
- ➡ Toucan: Swatch Editor

The company named itself to mimic its motto: "Creation on the fly." The suite has some heavy-duty capabilities, most of which I'd never need to accomplish the graphic editing I do. But it's cool that it's there and free when you need to create a complex graphic or multimedia component.

☑ **PRIVACY CHECK:** Their policy page makes their philosophy very clear:

Our Promise to You

Thank you for visiting Aviary. We know that you care how information about you is used and shared, and we appreciate your trust. Spam e-mail is the bane of the Internet and we won't have anything to do with it.

ALSO CHECK OUT

Sumo Paint (www.sumopaint.com): Another artist-community software site.

59

Google SketchUp

sketchup.google.com

3D MODELING FOR EVERYONE

The online world has a few free 3D-modeling tools, and my design friends tell me Google SketchUp is one of their favorites. The basic level is free to download, and they tell me it's easy to use, relatively speaking.

60

Vector Magic

www.vectormagic.com

$7.95

$7.95 a month for online application, or one-time fee of $295 for download.

 CONVERT BITMAP IMAGES TO VECTOR ART

Most digital graphics files look great on the screen but don't print out well. That's why your designer will ask for vector files instead of JPGs for a print job.

Vector Magic is an inexpensive way to convert a bitmap graphic into a scalable vector graphic. It's free to upload your graphic and try it out, and you get two free conversions once you sign up. Use the online version or download the application to your desktop.

ALSO CHECK OUT

 **Inkscape** (www.inkscape.org): An open source vector graphics editor that compares to Adobe Illustrator, Corel Draw, Freehand and Xara X. It's a free tool that allows you to edit and convert your vector graphics when you need high-resolution options for printing.

61

Caliper

bit.ly/U2Fcaliper

ACCURATELY MEASURE ANYTHING ON YOUR DESKTOP

When you're messing around with graphics for a Web page, newsletter or other online project, sometimes "I think that picture's the right size" just isn't good enough. Caliper takes the guessing out of your graphics sizing. It measures accurately down to one pixel.

A Caliper fan:

"For about 10 years I used a different measuring tool that just measured on a straight horizontal or vertical line. When I went looking for a new download, I was thrilled to find this one, which includes angles. Now it's perfect!"

Barbara Bailey, Web developer and online marketing/social media consultant for Visibility Consultants at visibilityconsultants.com.

62

Pixie

www.nattyware.com/pixie.php

FREE
For basic or go pro for $95.

 IDENTIFY SCREEN COLORS PIXEL BY PIXEL

Pixie is a tiny little program that allows you to identify colors on the screen so you can create graphics and documents that match. I use it all the time to replicate the colors from my clients' Web pages in the documents I create. You can keep it running all the time or simply call upon it when you need it. The default is that it sits on top of your other programs all the time. I find this annoying, so I turn it on and off. But it'll show the codes for the color of a pixel so you can replicate a color scheme. One of my favorites.

Comments from the Pixie people:

Back in 1999, we wanted an easy and convenient tool to handle colors: a simple tool with helpful, novel features to convert an otherwise annoying and complicated routine into a pleasant experience. Pixie is tiny, extremely easy to use, and it just works.

PLATFORMS: Windows

ALSO CHECK OUT

 **Color Cop** (colorcop.net): A favorite of Janet Miller, owner and publisher of the Clairemont Community News. www.clairemontcommunitynews.com.

 **ColorSchemer** tools (www.colorschemer.com): Color palette identification and help for both Mac and Windows, discovered by reader Melissa DiMatteo.

Color Palette Generator (www.degraeve.com/color-palette): Upload any picture to see an analysis of the colors. Great for using an image to inspire the look and feel of a website, report or brochure.

6
Screencapture Tools

Have you ever done a screencapture by pressing Print Screen, pasting it somewhere, trying to crop it, fighting with an arrow to try to make a point and then sending it off, hoping the recipient will understand what you meant?

Or, have you wanted to be able to walk someone through a procedure to demonstrate exactly what you need to communicate?

Screencapture tools will change your life. They allow you to capture the parts of the screen you want to show, add arrows and text and send them off with a few clicks of the mouse. You can also make a little movie that captures every click of your mouse so you can create demos or give specific feedback.

A quick note: this section might as well be called the Jing chapter, but people who read www.AskBethZ.com or attend my presentations will tell you that if all you do after reading this book is to download Jing (page 66), you've saved enough time and money to justify buying this book.

IN THIS CHAPTER:

Jing

jingproject.com

SCREENCAPTURES FOR FREE

One of my favorite free tools of all time is Jing, a little application from TechSmith, which makes the screencapture process insanely easy. Jing sits on your screen at all times in the form of a little yellow sun. You can click on the capture button to bring up crosshairs that allow you to capture the part of the screen you want. Then you can either create an image that you can add notes to, or a movie up to five minutes long! It rocks.

Another cool thing? Once you have the capture you want, you can save it to your computer or throw it up to your own private account at Screencast.com (page 153). You can even toss it up on YouTube, upload it to Facebook or Twitter or simply copy and paste it into a document.

I'm a sucker for a pretty interface, and Jing is king here. It sits on my desktop as a little glowing sun, and it comes to life when you scroll over it.

I've used Jing to point out typos, walk point-by-point through a client's document, upload graphics for my website and give designers direct feedback on a client's project. I also use Jing for itty-bitty webcasts and how-tos. Jing is great when you're working with a language or geographical barrier because you can use Jing to get your exact message across.

I can't take credit for discovering Jing. One of my clients, Chris Uschan from Omnipress (www.omnipress.com/chrisuschan), sent me the tool a couple of years ago. I have been a huge fan ever since, and I enthusiastically subscribe to the Pro edition.

66
—

The Jing folks told me that Jing was initially an internal tool that their development staff used:

We found it increasingly hard to provide feedback on product development via e-mail using words alone. A more robust screen recording tool like Camtasia Studio was a bit too cumbersome for what was meant to be a quick conversation via e-mail to discuss changes being implemented in product code or design review. It was with that revelation that we thought there might be "space" for a quick and simple tool that allows you to share information visually with the click of a button. And born was Jing Project.

Other people who love Jing:

"I can easily grab a 'picture' of anything, anywhere! I use it for everything ... instructions, examples, anytime I need to add a visual element to my document."

> *Debbie Pate-Newberry, association marketing and publications specialist with Communications by Design*

"It's free and it's easy. For screen grabs, just click the little sun on your desktop, choose what you want to include in the picture and save. For video, do the same thing: press Start and it records.

> *Peggy Gartin, self-proclaimed "writer, computer geek and rockstar-in-my-car," www.thepegisin.com*

"I use Jing to capture screen images of websites, guide clients to a specific place on demos and share screen images of anything to help tell a story or explain a product or feature."

> *Paul Wehking, vice president of strategic accounts, Omnipress, www.omnipress.com/paulwehking.*

67

ALSO CHECK OUT

 **GoView** (goview.com): From industry giant Citrix of GoToMeeting (page 187) and GoToMyPC (page 24), we have GoView. GoView is an easy video capture tool that records your screen and audio. Windows only, free, still in beta.

 **Snagit** (www.techsmith.com/screen-capture.asp): TechSmith's more functional paid tool with a one-time price of $49.95. Wonderful upgrade if you do a lot of screencaptures for both Mac and PC. Reader Beth Camero loves it. "SnagIt is fast, lightweight, configurable. I use this every day at least once." And reader Bryan Floyd (Synapse Wireless, www.synapse-wireless.com) says, "SnagIt is easy to use, good performance, reliable and fast. I use it to make a quick mock-up of ideas because it can create clear communication."

FastStone

www.faststone.org

FREE

Free for 30-days, then $19.95
for a lifetime license.

 ANOTHER WAY TO AVOID THE "PRINT SCREEN" BUTTON

FastStone Screen Capture comes in as an unobtrusive toolbar. You can capture windows, the full screen, a scrolling screen and a video with audio. In addition, when you capture something, you get a whole host of editing options to add a little more flair and details.

FastStone has a couple of extra handy tools like a screen magnifier plus a color picker (like Pixie, page 63). FastStone has a number of ways to export your capture, but I still prefer Jing's integration with Screencast.com (page 153), which allows you to simply toss your capture online into your library without having to actually upload it.

PLATFORMS: Windows

☑ **PRIVACY CHECK:** FastStone doesn't offer a privacy policy, but their Contact Us page says, "Our programs contain neither adware nor spyware!"

69
—

EasyPrompter

www.easyprompter.com

 FREE TELEPROMPTER TO SPEAK LIKE A PRO

Many people are using wonderful free tools such as Jing (page 66) to create online presentations. EasyPrompter is a quick and easy way to script your presentation so your "ums" and "wells" go away.

Paste your text into the teleprompter, then adjust the scrolling so it fits with the speed you'd like to talk. Most audio guys I've talked to said the biggest mistake is reading too quickly, so if you set the pace a little more slowly than you think it should be, you're probably on track.

EasyPrompter lets you use the online version, or you can download the program. It comes in as an HTML file, but the creator tells me it has full functionality.

ALSO CHECK OUT

 **CuePrompter** (www.cueprompter.com): 100 percent sponsored by ads.

CoSketch http://www.cosketch.com	**FREE**

SHARED WORKSPACE FOR BRAINSTORMING
AND COLLABORATING

Sometimes you don't need a full-blown flowchart or diagram and, instead, just want to quickly share any idea (or photo) on the fly. Enter CoSketch: a multi-user online whiteboard designed to quickly visualize and share your ideas as images. Anything you paint will show up for all other users in the room in real time and you're always just one click away from saving a sketch as an image for embedding on forums, blogs or anywhere else. Even better, it runs in all common browsers without plugins and installation is free. There's not even any need for registration.

ALSO CHECK OUT

Twiddla (www.twiddla.com): Web browse with a friend, and mark up what you see. A great way to collaborate on a website or other project.

CHEAP CASE STUDY	**A non-techy's favorite free tools for writers**
	Peter Bowerman

As a borderline Luddite, I had to chuckle at Beth's request for my "two-three top online tools that help you do your job better." As if I use SO many, I'd have to narrow the list to the top three. Funny. Cognizant of my techno-weenie tendencies, she cut me some slack, suggesting I just offer my top tips. I'll just pretend I don't feel like I'm Grandpa having my meat cut into small pieces for me …

Let's be honest. Like most businesspeople – or fellow humans for that matter – Google has to be our most valuable tool these days, but saying so would be monumentally cliché and unoriginal, something I'm oh-so-loathe to be. As such, here are few others:

 **Rodale's Synonym Finder:** And no, there's no "dot-com" on the end of that. It's a real book (*remember those?*), and one which, in my experience, renders the online thesauri a total joke. Seriously. This 3-inch-thick beauty (yes, I measured it) is hands-down, my MOST-used resource of all, online or otherwise. It'll just make your job of keeping your copy fresh and original that much easier, and make you stand out in the crowd.

Honorable Mention: *Woe Is I* – what Strunk and White's *Elements of Style* should/could have been with some creativity and lively writing on board.

 **www.rhymezone.com:** Okay, an online reference (arguably, because I haven't gotten around to buying a hard-cover rhyming dictionary ... soon). Regardless, this is a pretty cool tool. As someone who loves crafting slogans, taglines, names, headlines and book titles/subtitles as part of my copywriting offering, I need to know what rhymes with what. And even if those things aren't your bag, it can enhance the rhythm and cadence of any copy, making it (and by extension, you) that much more memorable.

A Trifecta of Weekly E-Newsletters

 *Marketing Minute* – from marketing guru Marcia Yudkin – as the name implies, it really does only take a minute: www.yudkin.com/markmin.htm.

 *Publicity Hound* – cool news, tips and case studies in the PR realm from PR maven Joan Stewart: www.publicityhound.com.

 *Easy Web Tips* – Web content/SEO pro Katherine Andes' bite-size morsels on Web usability. I always learn something: www.andesandassociates.com/Easy_Web_Tips_LHPX.html (then look right).

Peter Bowerman is the author of The Well-Fed Writer (2000), The Well-Fed Writer: Back For Seconds (2005), The Well-Fed Self-Publisher (2007) *and the 2009 edition of* The Well-Fed Writer. The Well-Fed Writer *books are how-to standards in the lucrative field of commercial freelancing – and the books that helped inspire Beth Ziesenis. Visit him on the Web at www.wellfedwriter.com.*

7
Photo and Font Tools

A picture may be worth a thousand words ... but what if those words were in a really groovy font?

There's a reason this chapter is one of the largest: I love the creative ways you can create graphics and throw in cool fonts to jazz up projects, presentations, websites and more.

I use tools in this chapter every week. From dafont (page 75) with hundreds of fun, free fonts, to BeFunky (page 78) with its easy special effects for photos, these tools bring something special to the look of any graphic or file.

IN THIS CHAPTER:

dafont

www.dafont.com

FREE

FUN, FUNKY AND FUNCTIONAL FONTS FOR YOUR GRAPHIC DESIGN NEEDS

Dafont.com is the best place on the Web to find fonts with a little pizazz to add a little something extra to your look and feel. I love putting my word or phrase into the custom preview box, the searching by theme (cartoon, curly, calligraphy, handwritten) to find just the right look. Most are free for personal use, and many are just plain free. An awesome resource for any do-it-yourself graphic designer.

CHEAP TIP:

Uncommon fonts rarely work well on websites or in HTML e-mails because the readers' computers probably don't have the font installed. You can always turn a heading or other text into a graphic that will maintain its integrity.

75

ALSO CHECK OUT

Font Squirrel (www.fontsquirrel.com): Free fonts for commercial use.

FontSpace (www.fontspace.com): Another cool font source with 13K+ fonts.

YourFonts
www.yourfonts.com

$9.95

For basic template, or $14.95 for two pages of characters.

MAKE HANDWRITTEN THANK-YOU NOTE
MARATHONS A THING OF THE PAST

For about ten bucks, you can create a font that mimics your own handwriting. You simply download their template, write in the characters, scan and upload the completed template and preview your font. You don't pay until the download, so if the preview isn't what you expected, you can try again.

Keep in mind that this technique works better on printed or block characters versus cursive. It may take you a couple of tries to fill in the template correctly. You may not fool your grandmother into thinking that you handwrote your Christmas update, but your own font can be a great touch for letters, thank-you notes, scrapbooks and journals.

JUST 'CUZ YOU CAN

Just for fun, check out **FlipMyText** (www.flipmytext.com). This silly service lets you reverse text, flip text, reverse words and otherwise mutilate pixels on a page to put a little zing into correspondence. It's eye-catching on Twitter (page 219), and a clever way of creating a hacker-proof password.

WhatTheFont

www.myfonts.com/WhatTheFont

FREE

IDENTIFY A MYSTERY FONT

Grab a graphic of a mystery font you'd love to identify, and upload it to WhatTheFont. The site will analyze the graphic and make recommendations to identify your font. If you don't find a match, try visiting the WhatTheFont Forum, where they say, "cloak-draped font enthusiasts around the world will help you out!"

The cool iPhone app lets you snap a picture of a mystery font and go through the quick identification process on your phone. Then you can send yourself e-mail summaries of the search results and font previews.

SMARTPHONE APPS: iPhone

ALSO CHECK OUT

Fonts.com (www.fonts.com): Click on Find Fonts, then scroll to Search by Site to identify a font from a sample.

TypeNavigator (typenav.fontshop.com): Interactive font search system.

CHEAP TIP:

If you're trying to embed the picture into a website or newsletter, the link they provide won't work. You need the URL of the actual picture, which you can usually find by right clicking on the graphic.

JUST 'CUZ YOU CAN

Ever need to just toss a picture up on the web? Pixlr, a favorite online graphics editor (page 58), created **imm.io** (imm.io), an easy little feature that allows you to instantly upload pictures. Just go to the site, choose your picture and pow ... it's online, complete with a link to share.

BeFunky

www.befunky.com

FREE

For basic level, and more features cost about $25 a year.

 FUN, EASY PHOTO EFFECTS

BeFunky Photo Effects allow everyday people to easily create fun and artsy digital images without the need for any technical knowledge. I'm particularly fond of their Cartoonizer effects, but the folks at BeFunky tell me people also love the Impressionist and Pop Art effects.

In the near future, they are adding more photo enhancement tools to remove wrinkles, adjust lighting and smooth or sharpen an image. Plus, they plan to offer users a chance to save their masterpieces as vector images.

SMARTPHONE APPS: iPhone and Android

ALSO CHECK OUT

 **SketchMyPhoto** (www.SketchMyPhoto.com): Many photo editors contain filters to create sketches from your photos, but I'm partial to this one. I uploaded my Twitter avatar, and Sketch My Photo came up with a perfect rendition. Saving your photo in a pretty good resolution is free. It's $5.95 to upgrade to a nicer version.

Crazy Online Generators

Sometimes a paper, a certificate, a newsletter or a Web page just needs a little something extra, like a clever sticky-note graphic with an important note, or maybe a humorous image to catch someone's eye.

Welcome to the world of online generators, where you can create informative, interesting or insane graphics with the perfect message for your audience.

I first discovered these when I needed a quick graphic that looked like a yellow sticky note, and I was blown away by the thousands of options I came across. Here's a sample of my favorite sources:

 **Official Seal Maker** (www.says-it.com/seal): Create a custom graphic, sign or logo with your own official seal. It's free to save the image on your computer, and you can create cool products with your seal for $1.50 to $21.55, which includes anything from a round button to stickers, hats or a beer stein.

 **Parody Motivator Generator** (diy.despair.com): Helps you create ridiculous (de)motivational posters. The graphics are free to download and $12.95 if you want a real poster.

 SignGenerator (www.signgenerator.org): The mother of all sign generator lists. Here's where you find the sticky-note templates as well as hundreds of other sign generators (church signs, shopping bag emblems, parking signs, panhandler signs and a billion others) that you can personalize as needed. Note: some of the generators involve off-color humor.

No privacy policy, but the first page has this FAQ:

Q: What's the scam to you offering these free generators?

A: No scam to download free pics, (however I will place one of our website addresses embedded in the image, small fee can remove this tag). It's not free to get a magnet or postcard either. Eventually I hope to earn a real income by charging some fees as being a "work-at-home dad" who has a young son.

 ## Wordle (www.wordle.net)

My sister, a science teacher in the Denver area, turned me on to Wordle. Wordle is a simple tool to create a "word cloud" graphic for any special event or report. Just provide a list of words (or a link to a site with an RSS feed), and Wordle will create a graphic with key words about your topic. You can tweak the colors, fonts, layouts and type sizes, or spend all day just clicking the random generation button. Here's a Wordle of some tools in this book.

iStockphoto.com

www.istockphoto.com

PRICE

Images start a little more than a buck per photo.

GREAT PRICES ON PROFESSIONAL STOCK PHOTOGRAPHY

If you've ever tried to purchase a professional photograph for a brochure, website or ad, you know how expensive they can be. That's why I am so glad repositories such as iStockphoto exist. Amateur and professional photographers, illustrators and multimedia artists offer great quality, royalty-free graphics at amazing prices – a credit will cost you a buck-fifty or less, and photos range from one credit to twenty-five, depending on the quality.

You can also buy audio, video and illustrations on the same credit system. I spend a couple hundred bucks a year to keep myself in credits, and I download graphics for my blog and client projects twice a month or more. iStockphoto is just one of the low-cost graphic providers out there, but I've been working with them for years, and I rarely come out empty-handed when I search for a particular look. Plus, they've partnered with Getty Images to provide more high-end media when needed.

ALSO CHECK OUT

PhotoXpress.com (www.photoxpress.com): A free subscription level allows up to 10 downloads a day from free photo bank. Other subscription levels start at $9.99.

Fotolia (www.fotolia.com): Free and low-cost images.

Flickr Creative Commons (www.flickr.com/creativecommons): Find photos that Flickr users are willing to share, with or without attribution.

81

CHEAP CASE STUDY	**A teacher's favorite resources**
	Sarah Ziesenis

As a high school teacher, I often look to the Internet for free resources. This year I assigned two projects that were Internet intensive: a brochure and a magazine.

 In order to create a brochure, students could choose to go to **www.mybrochuremaker.com** to easily make a free brochure.

 **www.discoveryeducation.com/freepuzzlemaker:** Another project had students create fun and educational puzzles using this free puzzle maker.

www.inspiration.com: I also create concept maps for students to fill in at. Although it is not free, they do have a free trial.

Now that you have so many great new graphics, where do you keep them? Download Google's **Picasa** (picasa.google.com) to organize, tag and catalog all the graphic files on your computer. "Open it, and it will find pictures on your computer, or tell you where to look," says contributor Bob Rausa, who uses digital photos to track and report the issues and progress of the boilers his company manufactures.

CHEAP TIP

Sarah Ziesenis, the sister of your very own nerdy best friend Beth Ziesenis, is a high school science teacher.

Gliffy

www.gliffy.com

FREE

Basic version is free, and Gliffy Premium is $5 a month for individuals.

 CREATE AND SHARE FLOW CHARTS AND DIAGRAMS

I think I can count on one hand the number of times I've needed a flowchart, so I was surprised at the number of quality diagramming collaboration tools I discovered.

One of my readers' favorites is Gliffy, a web-based tool that makes it easy for you to create, share and collaborate with diagrams. Gliffy has been around since 2005, and people use it for drawing and collaborating on floor plans, flowcharts, UML diagrams, network diagrams, SWOT analysis diagrams, business process models, technical drawings and more.

It's $25 a month for up to 10 users, with other packages available. Academic groups receive 50 percent discount on multi-user accounts.

ALSO CHECK OUT

 **Creately** (creately.com): Collaborate on flowcharts, wireframes, mind maps and diagrams.

83

Preceden

www.preceden.com

FREE

$29 for a lifetime membership. Free for teachers and students.

CREATE AN ATTRACTIVE TIMELINE

This handy little graphics tool lets you create a timeline for lesson planning, project scheduling, historical summaries and more. Your timeline lives online, and you can share the link with friends and colleagues.

ALSO CHECK OUT

Timetoast (www.timetoast.com): Different graphic interface, same concept.

TimeRime (www.timerime.com): Cool capabilities to add multimedia with free version as well as multiple pricing tiers for more advanced timelines.

84

8

Multimedia

Do you sometimes need a little music and movement, whether it's for a newsletter, a special presentation, a school project or something special for your website?

These tools bring audio, video and more to your projects. In this chapter you'll find one of the icons of the free and low-cost tools: Audacity (page 91), a robust audio editor that is backed by a passionate community of computer gurus who keep the program up to date and bug free.

This chapter also explores options for live broadcasting, which is about as multimedia as you can get. These free tools let you capture any moment on video and broadcast it live, even from your smartphone.

IN THIS CHAPTER:

86

Animoto

www.animoto.com

TURN PICTURES INTO A MULTIMEDIA EXTRAVAGANZA

In about five minutes, you can upload a few photos, choose a soundtrack and create a 30-second picture montage for a report, presentation or conference finale. Animoto is just plain cool, with an intuitive interface and fun graphics. It's won all kinds of awards including a Crunchy and a Webby, and you can even use it to create high-quality DVD videos.

Twitter god Brian Carter (briancarteryeah.com) uses it to "make videos quickly from images and text with free rockin' music." Another nice thing is that the music is there for your use. Artists upload their works to contribute to your masterpieces.

Thirty bucks lets you create unlimited length videos for a year. You can also buy one credit to produce one longer video for $3.

ALSO CHECK OUT

Flixtime (www.flixtime.com): 60-second video for free.

JUST 'CUZ YOU CAN

Bring a little humor into your report, newsletter or website with **ToonDoo** (www.toondoo.com), a comic strip generator. Stock graphics and an easy interface make it simple to create a few frames to illustrate a point and bring in a chuckle.

87

iSpring Free

www.ispringfree.com

FREE

For personal and private use. Commercial users must upgrade to the full version.

 CONVERT YOUR POWERPOINT TO FLASH

Download iSpring Free, a little PowerPoint add-in to convert your PowerPoint presentation into Flash with a push of a button in about a minute.

The converter keeps all your animations, transition effects, audio narrations and embedded video just where you have it. It creates a SWF file, making it easy to share via e-mail, link or on CD. The "i" in iSpring stands for "innovation," the company says. iSpring Free is a companion piece to the professional version.

88

Ustream
www.ustream.tv

STREAM LIVE VIDEO FROM ANY WEBCAM OR COMPATIBLE SMARTPHONE

Ustream is one of those free services that is almost beyond belief. You need a computer (or compatible smartphone), a webcam, a microphone and a high-speed Internet connection to be able to broadcast live online and interact with viewers via chat. Ustream has been around since 2006, and I discovered it in 2008 when I was one of the kabillions of people who was sucked in by the adorableness of the Shiba Imu Puppy Cam: adorable puppies, 24/7. These days more than 40 million people a month tune in to see live video.

During the holidays, I've used my iPhone to broadcast live video of my husband's family gathering back to my parents during their family gathering. You can also download Ustream Producer for free for advanced video editing, and Producer Pro ($199) does even more.

SMARTPHONE APPS:

➡ BlackBerry

➡ iPhone

➡ Android

☑ **PRIVACY CHECK:** Ustream is by design a very public forum. When you register, other members of Ustream can see your user name, comments and submissions. Ustream recommends you choose a user name that doesn't reveal personal info.

Ustream also says they will contact you with newsletters, marketing or promotional materials, but you can opt out from this correspondence. They also allow other members to send you e-mails through their system, but not directly. "Providing Other Member Information is voluntary and should correlate with the degree of interaction you want to have with Ustream.tv users.

89

We recommend that you guard your anonymity and sensitive information," the policy states. As with many organizations, they provide site demographic info to third parties, but your personal information is not sold or shared.

ALSO CHECK OUT

 **Justin.tv** (justin.tv): Started as a reality show with a guy named, uh, Justin, Justin.tv is another easy broadcasting service. Free with ads, and an ad-free pro account is $10 a month.

TinyChat (www.tinychat.com): Pull together up to 12 people by video and audio with a few keystrokes.

Audacity
audacity.sourceforge.net

THE ULTIMATE FREE AUDIO EDITOR

If I had to choose the free tool that I respect the most, award-winning Audacity would be at the top of the list. It's a fully functional, incredibly professional easy-to-use and multilingual audio editor and recorder. Downloading Audacity is essential for amateur multimedia creators who need to tweak audio for presentations. It's so solid a tool that I know many professionals who use it instead of (or in addition) to pricier alternatives.

| iSpeech
www.ispeech.org | **FREE**
For the basics with iSpeech advertising, and non-ad packages start at $29 a month. |

 CONVERT TEXT TO SPEECH

Frankly I'm one of those people who gets a little irritated when I hit a website and a movie comes up or audio starts playing. But my learning style lends itself to reading, not listening, and that's not true for everyone.

iSpeech is an online service that instantly converts text to speech. Cut and paste up to 50 words to give it a try with their basic service without registering. You can download or embed the resulting audio, and they say you can convert Web content, documents, your blog ... anything to speech.

WORTH THE PRICE

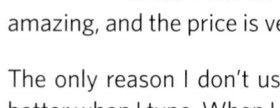**Dragon Naturally Speaking** (bit.ly/U2Fdragonspeaking): It works! No, really. You talk; it types. I bought a very early version, and it was horrible. I went hoarse trying to train the dang thing, especially since I started yelling at it after a while. But the new versions are amazing, and the price is very reasonable: about $80 for the smallest package.

The only reason I don't use it is that I found that my mind composes words better when I type. When I try to dictate a letter off the top of my head, I end up doing a lot of umm-ing and err-ing. So for me it's great when I need to dictate things that don't require much thought, such as a list of things to do or the notes from a meeting.

Want to test your typing skills against the software? Check out this demo: nuance.com/talk/swf/index.html.

Bonus! I love **Dragon Dictation**, a free iPhone app. Just tap the screen and talk, and it transcribes your words so you can text, e-mail and more.

Issuu

www.issuu.com

 CREATE AN ONLINE MAGAZINE OR CATALOG

Issuu won a slot in Time.com's 50 best websites of 2009. You can upload almost any type of document and create an online magazine, book or catalog that people can flip through. The graphics of the viewing interface will make you look like a pro, and it has built-in features that allow readers to share and download your files. I also like that you can create a little Issuu mini version to embed on your site.

ALSO CHECK OUT

 **Wobook** (www.wobook.com): Free for personal publications, and $13.50 for an upgraded account. Integrates with their iPhone app.

JUST 'CUZ YOU CAN

  **GoldMail:** Have you ever sent information via e-mail that you wish you could explain? (www.goldmail.com) can help. GoldMail lets you record audio voiceovers for PowerPoint slides and other documents to help your messages stand out. Speaker and author Mark Rosenberger (www.markrosenberger.com) loves the impact his GoldMail messages have on his audience. Free for basic level supported by ads. Many more features starting at $9.95 a month.

93

9

Small Business Tools

Don't small business owners and freelancers have enough to worry about?

They sure don't need to fret about a high-dollar tech budget when so many free and low-cost tools are around to help.

This chapter has tools to manage invoicing and your finances, keep in touch with contacts and find help when you need it. In addition, this chapter includes an essential tool to manage your online presence, plus a tool to help you keep track of the big picture.

IN THIS CHAPTER:

FreshBooks

www.freshbooks.com

 MANAGE YOUR BILLING ONLINE

FreshBooks is one of those ubiquitous tools that integrates into a number of systems you may already have, including MailChimp (page 37), Xpenser (page 99) and Wufoo (page 39). It includes time tracking, invoicing and other handy tools to help you keep the books and keep your company running.

Another cool thing is that you have access 24/7 from any browser or smartphone. I use a free accounting system, Microsoft Accounting Express, which is no longer supported. But I'm tethered to my desktop computer, which means I can't dash off an invoice if I'm not at the office. FreshBooks and other online accounting systems offer that access on the go.

Also, if you'd rather send invoices out through the regular mail, FreshBooks can do that, too. They'll even lick the stamp.

I like that they've been around since 2004, and they consistently show up on Top 10 technology lists.

SMARTPHONE APPS: BlackBerry and iPhone

ALSO CHECK OUT

 **Blinksale** (www.blinksale.com): Online billing with the ability to import clients from Basecamp (page 123). Prices start at six invoices a month for $6.

FreeAgent (www.freeagentcentral.com): Flat $20 a month to manage the books and invoice online.

 **Invotrak** (invotrak.com): Free version gives you two invoices a month for one client. Next level starts at $9 for up to 10 invoices and two clients.

 **LessAccounting** (lessaccounting.com): I like one of their taglines: "Provides a stress-free way to do your accounting, because your job title is not accountant." Starts at $12 a month to track invoices and expenses. Pay $100 monthly and they throw in quarterly help from a real-live bookkeeper.

 **Paymo Time Tracking and Invoicing** (www.paymo.biz): Free for freelancers, or $3.99 per employee per month.

  **Time Stamp** (www.syntap.com/products_timestamp.htm): If you just need a time tracker, Web developer and social media consultant Barbara Bailey (visibilityconsultants.com) likes Time Stamp, a donationware download that tracks time and calculates cost for the time. Windows only, and last version verification was for Windows XP.

 **WorkflowMax** (www.workflowmax.com): This tool integrates project management, invoicing and time tracking and helps you measure how productive a team is. One user is $15 a month, and a small office of up to five people is $49. Also includes a handy iPhone app.

 **Xero** (www.xero.com): An international version that gives you access to bank transactions, invoices and reports – anytime you need it, anywhere in the world. Includes real-time, multi-currency capabilities. Pricing starts at $19 monthly.

FastDue

www.fastdue.com

 **FREE ONLINE ACCOUNTING WITH CONTRACT TEMPLATE LIBRARY**

Ever need to just dash off a note or an invoice or a complaint quickly – without having to take time to actually format it and figure out what it needs to say?

FastDue is the perfect place to find quality invoices and other templates for all kinds of business needs. FastDue lets freelancers, entrepreneurs, start-ups, small offices and home offices and professionals handle their invoicing, create legal agreements, track their expenses and perform other business functions easily online – avoiding unnecessary and costly involvement with complicated software or professional services.

Why did they create it? As they say:

Our original goal was to help freelancers and small businesses collect more efficiently, without having to use collection agencies. However, based on the things users were telling us about what they could use to run their businesses, our scope expanded to include today's balanced set of tools for managing a variety of necessary business functions.

FastDue Plus costs $9.95 a month and gives you more templates and the ability to brand your documents.

SMARTPHONE APPS: iPhone

Xpenser
xpenser.com

 EASILY KEEP TRACK OF YOUR EXPENSES

Almost every professional I know needs to keep track of expenses sometime or another. Just pick up your phone and text "Taxi San Francisco 36" to the program, and the system will record your taxi trip in San Francisco and the date online in a report with all your other expenses. You can also send expenses in via e-mail, iPhone, Twitter, IM and more. Xpenser also tracks your mileage and can convert currency automatically.

Once you look at your report online, you can export it into Excel or an accounting system (such as FreshBooks, page 96).

☑ **PRIVACY CHECK:** Xpenser says right off that they won't share your information unless, "instructed by you; required by law; or required to enforce our terms of service, prevent fraud or un-lawful activity, ensure the security of our network and services, or maintain our ability to conduct business in good faith." They note that they use cookies "to make our site easier to use," but they will not share information collected by the cookie. Xpenser notes that you may access their services through another provider (such as when you send in an expense via Twitter), and that your privacy in those cases will depend on the privacy policies of the other services.

99

Salesforce.com www.salesforce.com	**$5** *Basic contact management for up to five users is $5 a month. More features come with the next level at $25.*

 TRACK LEADS, CONTACTS AND CONTRACTS

When I quit my job in sales, I almost called Salesforce.com and begged them for a job. I love this organization. Not only have they revolutionized customer relationship management (CRM) affordability for small businesses, they run the Salesforce Foundation, whose philosophy is to give back to the community: 1 percent in time by encouraging their employees to volunteer, 1 percent in donations with free services for qualifying nonprofits and 1 percent in profits.

Salesforce.com brings organized, professional CRM to the little people. At certain price levels, you can do everything from manage your contacts, track your communications and create e-mail campaigns, to monitor sales (both the process and the signed contracts) and set up project management tools. In addition, they have hundreds of integrations in their AppExchange, many of which are in this book. They help people get the most out of their service with live events as well as webinars and other resources.

ALSO CHECK OUT

 **SugarCRM** (www.sugarcrm.com): The community level for this CRM is free. The next level starts at $360 a year for many more features.

 **Timetonote** (www.timetonote.com): Collaborate and share contacts with colleagues, and keep track of communications, notes, tasks, projects and more. Free for up to 2 team members, 10 projects and 250 contacts. The Premium level is $20 a month for unlimited members, projects and contacts.

100

Elance

www.elance.com

$50

Depends on project.
$50 minimum.

FREELANCER DATABASE FOR EVERY ITEM ON YOUR TO-DO LIST

If you're a small business owner or even a professional with a small staff, you're going to love Elance. Freelancers and small businesses from all around the world are waiting to help you on Elance. All you need to do to hire a pro is to create a project and put it out for bids. You can find providers who meet your needs and invite them specifically to bid on your projects, or you can wait and see who finds you. The cool thing about Elance (besides the very affordable prices you can find) is that you don't release payment until you're satisfied, so you can guard against a flighty freelancer.

ALSO CHECK OUT

Guru.com (www.guru.com): Another community of experts with more than a million registered users.

CHEAP CASE STUDY	**Using Elance to brand a company**
	Jaime Cevallos

When you are starting a new company, I think it is important to *develop* a professional looking logo that you can be proud of. Think of a website without a logo. The most popular website of all, Google, has almost nothing else on the home page. Hopefully, you will have plenty of visitors to your website and offering your business cards daily. You want to feel confident in your branding from the beginning.

So as long as you have created a catchy name for your company, it's time to create a logo. When I first started *The Swing Mechanic*, I hired a local Web designer to make my logo. I had the idea in my head; I just needed a professional to make it look sharp. The local designer charged me $500, took five weeks to complete it, and the final product was a disaster.

Then I hired a designer on Elance.com. I provided a description of the logo, just as I did for the local designer, and for just $90 I had a professional looking logo the very next morning – less than 2 days after posting the project. I still use the same logo today.

CHEAP TIP

When getting a logo created, ask for many variations for the final deliverable. For example, I asked for the designer to provide me with just the bat and just *The Swing Mechanic* in PDF, JPG and PNG formats.

Jaime Cevallos, inventor of the MP30 and MP28 Training Bats and author of Positional Hitting. *Visit him on the Web at www.theswingmechanic.com.*

LogoMyWay
www.logomyway.com

$200

Minimum $200 contest prize. The more you offer, the more ideas you'll get. I received ideas from more than 60 designers.

NEW IDEAS TO SPRUCE UP AN OLD LOGO

Hiring someone to design a logo is fairly straightforward if you know what you want. Find a good designer, give them your idea and let them hone in on the perfect graphic, and it'll cost you a few hundred bucks.

But it's when you don't know what you want that you may run into some trouble. There are excellent graphic designers out there who can take you through a process to brand your company or event and create a logo. But you could (and should) pay for their expertise, and that could be pricey.

I give that warning because this next low-cost tool for a business is a little controversial in the design world. On sites like LogoMyWay, you upload a description of the graphic you need and establish a contest prize (usually $200 bucks or more) for a winning logo. Then literally thousands of designers can submit ideas for your logo. You can keep the contest open for a week or two and give feedback along the way so your favorite ideas get the tweaks they need to help you pick a winner.

I used this service to create a new logo for Avenue Z Writing Solutions when I revamped my website (www.avenuez.net). I was pulled aside by a designer friend who told me that designers who use these sites can be guilty of plagiarism and copyright violation when they submit designs. She also told me that recommending these types of services devalues the work that mainstream graphic designers can do for a company. She's right. On both counts. But I still love the idea of seeing all kinds of ideas for your new look, and I'd do this again.

ALSO CHECK OUT

crowdSPRING (www.crowdspring.com): Another home for affordable designs and a favorite of Gini Dietrich, the author of *Spin Sucks* and founder and CEO of the non-traditional marketing firm Arment Dietrich (armentdietrich.com).

Get Satisfaction

www.getsatisfaction.com

WE ALL NEED A LITTLE SATISFACTION

Get Satisfaction allows you to setup a feedback mechanism for your product or service. Set up an account and link it to your site, and customers, community members and any other interested parties can pop in and leave valuable tips, ideas, feedback and constructive criticism.

ALSO CHECK OUT

Trackur (www.trackur.com): Monitor your reputation in social media. Free account gives you one search with unlimited results. Other levels start at $18 a month.

Google Alerts www.google.com/alerts	**FREE**

TRACK YOUR WEB PRESENCE

If you are a professional, you need to be using Google Alerts. With Google Alerts, you can track keywords in the Web world in news articles, blogs and other citations. Set them up for your company's name, your name, even hot keywords in your field. You will receive e-mails that list places your alerts were mentioned on the Web.

I set them up for my last name, my company and keywords related to my clients. Every mention is aggregated and delivered via e-mail. This saves me the hassle of doing "ego searches."

THE Jessica Smith of @JessicaKnows on Twitter said, "Google Alerts lets me keep tracking what people are saying about me so I can respond (or not) as needed." And Meg Tully, Nonprofit Know How (www.npfknowhow.com) owner, added, "Our association can't pay for a clipping service, so this at least keeps us informed about the biggest issues out there. Much of the info is not relevant to exactly what I'm looking for, but this has been a great way to find out about the big issues."

105

ALSO CHECK OUT

Sendible (sendible.com): Market your business and monitor your brand in your social media networks.

PlanHQ

www.planhq.com

$9

Plans start at $9 a month for three members or 10 goals and go up to unlimited goals and members for $49 a month.

 **DON'T FAIL TO PLAN**

Dallon Christensen is a small business owner who prides himself on running his company with free and low-cost tools (see his Cheap Case Study on page 189). He considers PlanHQ an essential tool to aid in the growth of his company.

PlanHQ is a web-based business plan tool that helps you convert your ideas for your business into a real plan, giving you a dynamic and up-to-date overview of where you're going and how you're tracking.

You turn your strategic goals into real tasks, then you track your progress towards achieving those goals. Your business colleagues contribute and share tasks with the system. PlanHQ would work well for entrepreneurs, startups and growing businesses – really anyone organized enough to make a plan for growing their business (this eliminates me – I've never written a business plan in my life).

106

10

Website and Blogging Tools

Don't you think whether you're a student, a small business owner or an employee, chances are you might need to manage a website?

If you're not a Web designer, building and maintaining a site can be incredibly annoying, frustrating and downright miserable.

But these free and low-cost tools can help. Use them to build your site, add little touches, keep track of the traffic and more. In addition, tools such as WordPress (page 110) will open up a whole host of new free and low-cost add-ons and plug-ins to help you maintain and enhance your site.

IN THIS CHAPTER:

108

SnapPages

www.snappages.com

FREE

Personal sites are free, and business sites are $8 a month, including hosting.

 QUICK WEBSITES EVEN YOUR GRANDMA CAN CREATE

My assistant Claire took a liking to this tool. SnapPages gives you all the tools you need to create your very own website. Start with a theme, but customize the heck out of it. Add blog posts, widgets and pictures (the picture capabilities are even cooler!). Perhaps if I had known about SnapPages, I would have built my site there instead of having it done professionally.

ALSO CHECK OUT

 **GRSites** (www.grsites.com): Buy a five-day pass with GRSites for $10 (or a fourteen-day pass for $7.95) to design your own site without having to know a single thing about HTML. Then grab the code and create your own site with another host.

JUST 'CUZ YOU CAN

 If you ever want to run a contest on your blog or site, **ContestMachine** (contestmachine.com) makes it easy. The system takes care of the details, from collecting entries to notifying winners. You just need to embed the widget and send the prize. Contest prices start at $9.95 a month for unlimited entries of up to four contests per month.

109

WordPress.com
www.wordpress.com

FREE

If you host it yourself, you'll pay hosting fees, probably $7-14 a month, depending on your service.

 THE ULTIMATE IN BLOG SOFTWARE

When it comes to blogs, you just can't get better than WordPress. There's a reason it's the most popular blog software out there. It's easy to use, very flexible and includes thousands of free plug-ins to make your blog incredibly professional, attractive and useable.

CHEAP TIP:
Many, many sites today use WordPress to create a professional look. It's a blog, but it won't feel like one. Visit www.askbethz.com for samples.

You can go one of two routes to use WordPress. If you sign up for a free one at WordPress.com, you'll get a site (in minutes!) with a URL like www.YourSite.wordpress.com. Or you can go to any number of hosting companies that have made it super easy for you to launch your own WordPress blog from their site and keep it updated.

110

After you have a site, you can browse a kabillion (yes ... a KA-BILLION!) free templates to pick out the one that best represents the look you want to convey, or you can have someone design one for you (see Elance for freelancers, page 101). I've done it both ways, but I like to start with an established template to cut down on design and development time.

I'm not the only one who loves WordPress. One reader wrote:

"WordPress is easy to use, and it seems to be endless because of its plugins and stellar community. It is where I do my work. For some reason, my writing flows out of me when I'm using this software in a way that it doesn't flow anywhere else." And reader Beth Camero says she uses it on several personal blogs and two work blogs because "it's updated regularly, is secure and has a great interface."

SMARTPHONE APPS: BlackBerry and iPhone

ALSO CHECK OUT

 **Penzu** (penzu.com): Now here's a switch ... Penzu is an online blog-type service that you can keep private! All the other blogs in the world are out there so you can share your thoughts, but Penzu lets you create a private journal for your eyes only, though you can choose to share with others. *PC Magazine* gave it props for being some of the best free software of 2009. Free for the basic plan, and if you go Pro for $19 a year, they donate some of the proceeds to charities that support literacy.

 **Posterous** (posterous.com): Can blogging get any easier? Without visiting the site, simply e-mail post@posterous.com, and they post what you've e-mailed. You can then claim a site of your own and keep posting to it. It even adds your pictures, videos, documents ... anything you attach to the e-mail. Posterous also works with Twitter, WordPress and Facebook.

 **Tumblr** (www.tumblr.com): The favorite easy blogging platform of Jessica Smith, aka @JessicaKnows on Twitter. Tumblr even lets you phone in an audio post.

JUST 'CUZ YOU CAN

 **Balsamiq Mockups** (www.balsamiq.com/products/mockups): The $79 software carries a hefty pricetag for a free and low-cost tools book, and it's a little techy-sounding as well. But gosh ... this tool looks awesome. You draw out a frame with all the features you want on a Web page with just a few clicks. When I say "you," I do mean you. It is easy to use and understand, and I could totally see me using this tool to make a demo of what I'd like to see in my next site.

The version available now is downloadable, but they should be launching the online version soon, and that one will work on a subscription model. Thus, perhaps you can buy a month's subscription to help you with your next project. They also mentioned the "donate a TON of licenses to nonprofits and other do-gooders," so it doesn't hurt to ask them for a favor if you fall into that category.

Where did the name come from? The owners told me, and it's kinda funny:

Balsamic vinegar, the high-end, the "aged for 25+ years" kind, has a lot in common with what we want our software to be: rich, smooth, pleasurable, expensive. OK our software is actually very affordable but we still want it to feel like a treat! Like a fine balsamic vinegar, our software adds flavor to something else (in our case Web apps), requires craftmanship and is made in Italy!

embedit.in

embedit.in

FREE

EMBED DOCUMENTS IN YOUR SITE AND
TRACK VIEWS, DOWNLOADS AND MORE

Embedit.in, now a part of Box.net (page 151), allows you to embed a file into your website and track the traffic, collect feedback and more.

What's super cool about this service is that you can sweep a website where you've linked to a bunch of documents with their tool called Sitewide (embedit. in/sitewide) to convert all your document links into embedded documents.

When they're embedded, clicking on the link has the document pop up in a new screen with an attractive interface. Visitors can share it, scroll through it, download it and print it.

ALSO CHECK OUT

Backboard (www.getbackboard.com): Get feedback on documents and sites with another tool from embedit.in's team.

JUST 'CUZ YOU CAN

This free tool is very specialized for IT folks, but it's such a good deal I just had to mention it. Tell your IT friends about **Spiceworks Network Management** (www.spiceworks.com), IT management software designed for IT pros who manage networks with up to 1,000 devices. They have more than a million IT pros using it worldwide. It combines inventory, monitoring, troubleshooting, reporting, help desk and a user community into one easy-to-use application. The founders told me the name came from the need to "spice IT up!" since the area of IT utilities was so dang boring.

# Chartbeat chartbeat.com	**$9.95** *A month to monitor up to five sites. Well worth the price.*

 REAL-TIME WEBSITE ANALYTICS

I first discovered Chartbeat when Ashton Kutcher and CNN were competing to be the first Twitter account with one million followers. Chartbeat showed the race live, and I was hooked.

For about 10 bucks a month, you can monitor the traffic on up to five websites in real time. I mean really real. It shows how many people are visiting, whether they're new or returning, what pages they are on, how long it took for their pages to load, who is talking about you on Twitter, where they live ... everything you might want to know.

On sites with very moderate traffic (like mine when I haven't posted a new free tool lately), it can be incredibly boring. But when I send out a newsletter or one of my tools goes viral for a few minutes on Twitter, I can monitor the "stickiness" of my site. Do they visit just one page or click around for a few? How long are they hanging out?

You can set up alerts so you get a text when a certain number of people visit your site at once, and the service sends you e-mails (or texts, your choice) when your site is down (which happens more than you know). The Chartbeat folks told me they chose the name because "Chartbeat is the heart beat of your site, and we like charts!"

SMARTPHONE APPS: iPhone

ALSO CHECK OUT

 **Clicky** (www.getclicky.com): Get one website (with basic features) for free if your total daily views are under 3,000. The next level gives you three sites and 10,000 hits for $4.99 a month or about $30 a year.

CHEAP CASE STUDY	**Revamping a website with low-cost tools**
	Beth Ziesenis

In 2009 I overhauled the look and feel of my main company, Avenue Z Writing Solutions (www.avenuez.net). The complete makeover of the Avenue Z site with the new logo was affordable and quick to launch thanks to a few great tools.

 **WordPress Professional Templates** (www.themeforest.net): I'm a big fan of not inventing wheels. When I started looking for a site, I surfed free and low-cost site templates that my designer could customize. The template for my new site cost $25 and saved hours in labor.

 **Logo Contest Sites** (www.logomyway.com): For $200, more than 60 designers submitted ideas for the new logo. I found out later that many professional designers frown upon these contests because of the risk for copyright infringement and the general devaluing of their profession. But if you need a quick logo for a particular event, I loved the easy process and the great results. Bonus: The winning designer created a business card design plus letterhead for another $75. (See page 103.)

 **Freelance Designers** (www.elance.com): I actually hired a talented (and very reasonably priced!) designer I met through Twitter, but Elance is worth a mention. You can create a project on Elance and collect bids from freelancers all over the world. A company on Elance designed my first site for $180, and I've used the service for several other projects. (See page 101.)

Down for everyone or just me?

downforeveryoneorjustme.com

FREE

 **CHECK WEBSITE STATUS**

Ever have that horrible feeling when you go to your site and it's down? HOW LONG HAS IT BEEN LIKE THIS? HOW BAD IS IT? One time I was showing my client his new site, and bleh! It was down! We pasted his Web address into Downforeveryoneorjustme.com and discovered that it was just a problem with my connection, not his site.

Down for everyone or just me? is a service of Site5 Web hosting (www.site5.com). When you find out if your site is down, Site5 flashes a message, "We guarantee our uptime! Switch to Site5 hosting!" Sometimes I'm tempted to take them up on their offer.

116

Google Analytics

www.google.com/analytics

FREE

 THE VERY, VERY BEST FREE SITE TRAFFIC TOOL

I almost hesitate to include Google Analytics in this book because it's such a fantastic tool and it's been around so long that I can't imagine you don't know about it.

Just visit the homepage, log in and install the code that the system generates into your website. Within minutes, you'll be receiving some of the most comprehensive statistics about your website traffic that you will ever receive. You'll discover:

➡ How people find your site

➡ How often they visit

➡ Where they hang out

➡ What page they leave from

➡ Where your visitors come from, and so much more

I could write a whole chapter on their statistics. In fact, a search on Amazon.com turned up almost 200 books that include info about Google Analytics, several of them dedicated to just that topic! Analytics is a companion to Google AdWords, the money machine that earns Google a kabillion dollars a year.

Bottom line: If you have a website, you should have Google Analytics.

117

☑ **PRIVACY CHECK:** Google lives by five policy principles that describe how they handle your information and privacy when you use any of their services. They state that Google will:

➡ *Use information to provide our users with valuable products and services.*

➡ *Develop products that reflect strong privacy standards and practices.*

➡ *Make the collection of personal information transparent.*

➡ *Give users meaningful choices to protect their privacy.*

➡ *Be a responsible steward of the information we hold.*

When they first released Google Buzz, Google received criticism because users' contacts were by default available for anyone to see, but they quickly changed that.

Cool Little Website Tools

Here's my little collection of places you can go to get special touches for your site. They're all free and easy to use for those of us who are website impaired.

 **Cool Text** (cooltext.com): Need a quick button for your site? I love this free tool. Cool Text creates simple logos and buttons in a few minutes. I'm more fond of the buttons than I am the logos, but they're both worth a few minutes of experimentation.

☑ **PRIVACY CHECK:** Cool Text runs on ads, and they do not collect any personal information from you to use their site. If you voluntarily provide personal information to an ad (such as filling out a survey or putting in your zip code), Cool Text will collect this info to share with the advertiser. In general, they use aggregate information (like the type of stats you can get from Google Analytics (page 117) to tell advertisers the demographics of the site's visitors. They also install a cookie the first time you visit to target ads better.

 **Da Button Factory** (www.dabuttonfactory.com): Another quick and free button generator.

 **favicon.cc** (www.favicon.cc): Favicons are those tiny graphics in the tabs when you open a Web page. If you don't have one for your site, you'll get a little blank page graphic, and that's no longer the cool thing to do. Favicon.ico Generator will help you generate the tiny 16x16 pixel graphic – upload a graphic or paint your own.

 **Hidetext.net** (hidetext.net): Spammers sweep websites to collect e-mail addresses, so many people resort to formatting their contact info as something like: beth (at) askbethz (dot) com. Hidetext.net helps you turn your e-mail address into a graphic so it can't be detected. Just type in your e-mail address or any other text such as passwords or personal messages, and Hidetext converts it to a graphic that you can download or drag and drop.

 **Web Graphics Maker** (en.web-graphics-maker.com): Web Graphics Maker is an old-school but handy site to create quick-and-easy graphics for your Webpage. Use it for lines, backgrounds and bullets for your website or other graphic needs.

11

Project Management Tools

Didn't project management used to be a very complicated thing?

After all companies would hire project managers, frequently people with advanced degrees who were trained to coordinate with all the doers and approvers and money-spenders on a project to get work completed on time and on budget. The projects they talked about were BIG ones: building a rocket, buying a company, rolling out a new product. The project manager would use specialized software (such as Microsoft Project) to identify resources, tasks, timetables and the like, and the project manager would take care of assigning the jobs and checking up on people. There were these mysterious graphics called Gantt charts that were supposed to show the progress of the project, but really only the project manager knew how to create and read them.

But more and more smaller organizations just needed to figure out how to coordinate projects that didn't involve rocket scientists. They needed to bring together designers, committee members and the department heads to revamp the website. They needed to organize a conference or collaborate on an end-of-the-year report for the board.

Thus began an era of what I like to call "Project Management for the Rest of Us." Software companies used the Web as a gathering place for to-do lists, action items, resource libraries and communication. Setting up the project was easy to do for the average computer user, and groups could break down the projects into their components to make sure everyone did his part.

These days dozens of companies now offer fairly low-cost ways for groups to work together remotely and in the office to get things done. This section covers a variety of vendors, from the pioneers in this space to the startups.

IN THIS CHAPTER:

Basecamp

basecamphq.com

THE PIONEER IN ONLINE PROJECT MANAGEMENT

I have to start with the project management system that really kicked off the new trend. In 2004, a company called 37signals started creating online project management systems, primarily for the Web design industry. Basecamp has evolved to be one of the most popular Web-based project collaboration tool to share files, meet deadlines, assign tasks, centralize feedback and finish what you start.

Basecamp is now integrated with a whole host of other systems, including time-tracking software, social networks, mobile phones, invoicing software and much more. All the systems update each other and keep everyone on track.

Freelance technical writer Mark McClure (samuraiwriter.com/blog) says, "I hate managing copywriting assignments using e-mail attachments." He sets up one Basecamp project per client and stores all the copy online, along with task lists and reminders.

SMARTPHONE APPS: iPhone

123

ALSO CHECK OUT

 **Smartsheet** (www.smartsheet.com): The project management tool based on the spreadsheet system. Starts at $9.95 a month. Cool beans feature: your tasks integrate directly with livework (www.livework.com), a database of virtual outsourcing groups who can help with your tasks.

 **CreativePro Office** (www.creativeprooffice.com): The project management tool of choice for Web designer and marketing consultant Julie Mazziotta. Starts at $5 per month for one user.

 **GanttProject** (www.ganttproject.biz): Long for Gantt charts? Have no fear. Ganttproject is a free download for Mac, PC and Linux platforms.

 **Qtask** (www.qtask.com): Collaboration and project management for $9.95 per user per month.

Pelotonics

www.pelotonics.com

FREE

Free for two projects and up to 50MB of documents with unlimited users. Next level is $9 a month for 1GB storage and up to five projects.

AN ALTERNATIVE TO BASECAMP

I have a soft spot for Pelotonics for a few reasons. My friend Troy Malone started developing Pelotonics while we were working together at another company. Our team was using Basecamp to manage projects, and Troy wanted more features and a simpler interface from Basecamp. So he developed his own product, and I've been watching them grow ever since.

In cycling, riders work together in a peloton to maximize efficiency, and they expend about 30 percent less energy in the pack than when they ride alone. That's the theory behind the group project management in Pelotonics.

Pelotonics provides your team with a trusted system to securely manage communications, organize files and assign and track deliverables. It's integrated with both Google Docs (page 195) and Evernote (page 28). Pelotonics is almost out of beta, and they'll be adding mobile apps and more integrations soon.

125

Scrumy

scrumy.com

FREE

Basic service is free, and the Pro version costs $7 a month or $60 a year.

DID YOU HEAR THE PROJECT MANAGEMENT JOKE ABOUT THE PIG AND THE CHICKEN?

When I first read the name of this company, I thought it was pronounced "screw-me," which didn't sound like a wonderful name for a project management system. But it actually comes from "Scrum," a project management process.

According to Wikipedia, Scrum has two types of actors in a project management process, "pigs" and "chickens." This comes from a joke:

A pig and a chicken are walking down a road. The chicken looks at the pig and says, "Hey, why don't we open a restaurant?" The pig looks back at the chicken and says, "Good idea, what do you want to call it?" The chicken thinks about it and says, "Why don't we call it 'Ham and Eggs'?" "I don't think so," says the pig, "I'd be committed, but you'd only be involved."

In other words, in the Scrum process, a "pig" is a leader who is depending on the project to work, and a "chicken" is interested in the project but its success or failure doesn't really affect him.

What does that have to do with Scrumy? Not much, but I just had to share that joke.

Scrumy is very, very simple to set up and understand. You don't even have to go to the site to get started. Simply type "scrumy/[NAME YOUR PROJECT]" into an address bar, and the next page you'll see is an empty project, ready for the first tasks.

☑ **PRIVACY CHECK:** I didn't see a privacy policy on their site or blog. That's a little worrisome. As far as I can see, if you don't have a Pro account (starting at $7 a month), anyone who has your URL can see your projects and progress. Pro accounts allow you to password protect your site.

126

Tom's Planner

www.tomsplanner.com

FREE

Free for a personal account.

 **PROJECT MANAGEMENT FOR PEOPLE WHO LOVE GANTT CHARTS**

You gotta love a service that is named after a guy named Tom. Tom's Planner is an online project planning visualization system that allows anyone to easily create, share and publish online planning schedules (Gantt charts) with drag-and-drop simplicity without having to figure out Microsoft Project.

I love the colorful user interface and the right-click capabilities in any chart. Take a look at their templates to see examples of how people can use Tom's Planner for wedding planning, event planning, construction projects and more.

ProofHQ

www.proofhq.com

 **GET CLIENTS TO COMMIT TO A FINAL DRAFT**

Do you struggle with your clients to get them to actually approve a final version? I know sometimes I submit a large project, and it takes weeks (months?) to know if we're actually done.

ProofHQ takes you and your client through a systematic approval process. You upload a draft, invite your client to give feedback, document the revisions and work toward getting your client to say, "Yes. This is perfect. We're done." The tool integrates with Basecamp and other project management tools to give you a full-featured project management system.

CHEAP CASE STUDY

Sometimes you get what you pay for

Tom McCallum

As a Scot, being frugal is something that is pretty deeply ingrained for me, so I certainly have tried and used more than my fair share of freeware. Having said that, I'd suggest you don't lock yourself into a mantra of avoiding paying for software subscriptions at all costs. Consider what your time is truly worth. Now, be honest with yourself, wouldn't paying for a few good licenses or services not be worth more to you than that next latte?

In addition to the returns on your small investments, software companies (such as the evangelizing crew at 37Signals (see Basecamp, page 123) are increasingly working out that their business model should include (gasp!) charging for their product, so if you insist on using only "freeware," you are going to miss out on some pretty cool stuff that can definitely make life easier.

A few of my own favorites … some free, some paid:

Google Apps (page 146): For small businesses, this is still free. If you like Gmail but want your own domain, this is THE best free app out there.

RoboForm (page 174): Securely saves website logins. When I was "a PC," I had over 700 logins saved. That's a lot of passwords I didn't have to remember.

Dropbox (page 151): The next generation won't remember what "FTP" was. Great service for data sharing. Free to 2GB (more free space for referring friends), cheap beyond that.

Evernote (page 28): $5 per month to make organizing your life SO much easier.

TeuxDeux (page 133): An exquisitely simple (and free) to-do list.

Backupify (page 156): If you use software services, use this to back them up (Twitter, Google Docs, WordPress and more). Free up to 2GB, cheap beyond that.

Seatguru (page 23): If you travel a lot, making life on the road flow easier is worth a lot to you, but this one is free and does what the title says.

ExpertFlyer (page 23): $9.95 per month gives you an awesome tool for finding out where those airline frequent flyer award seats are hiding, and even alerting you when new seats are released. Essential for frequent travelers and worth far more than the price.

I closed with two travel tools because in my experience "road warriors" have turned using a whole bunch of free and/or cheap tools and services to make their life easier into a fine art. We could all learn from that.

Tom McCallum is a consultant, coach and mentor for McCallum Solutions (mccallumsolutions.com) in the Cayman Islands.

12

To-Do Lists and Reminders

Are all of your plates starting to spin out of control?

I used to use the reminders and task-list features of Microsoft Outlook to try to keep track of everything I had to do. I carefully logged them all. But sooner or later (usually sooner), the list ended up out of control, and my organizational system collapsed.

These free and low-cost to-do lists are designed to help you get organized and stay on top of all your tasks. You can choose tools that color code, integrate with other tools and make your list your own. This chapter also includes some handy reminder tools that convert your tickler file items into actionable messages that get things done.

So which is my favorite to-do list? I have a confession. I've eschewed all the electronic helpers in favor of good old pen and paper. I prefer spiral-bound steno pads (recycled paper, of course). I'm pretty much lost each day until I write the date on the top of the page and make my list. (I'm not the only one who goes retro when it comes to free tools sometimes. Check out the free tools for writers from author Peter Bowerman, page 71.)

IN THIS CHAPTER:

Remember The Milk

www.rememberthemilk.com

A CLASSIC IN ONLINE TO-DO LISTS

Based on the number of accolades, integrations and generally good press, I consider Remember The Milk one of the leaders in the very crowded to-do list space. It integrates with some of my favorite tools including Twitter (page 219). In April 2010 they passed the 2 million mark for RTM fans, and they continue to grow.

As with many of these to-do lists, RTM makes it easy to make lists, organize them, subdivide them and get things done. You can share your online lists with others, and everyone can work together toward the common goal.

Another cool thing is that RTM can send you reminders about due dates anywhere you hang out: e-mail, SMS and instant messenger, including AIM, Gadu-Gadu, Google Talk, ICQ, Jabber, MSN, Skype and Yahoo.

SMARTPHONE APPS:

➡ BlackBerry

➡ iPhone

➡ Android

➡ iPhone Touch

ALSO CHECK OUT

 **DoitDoitDone!** (www.doitdoitdone.com): A to-do list with no registration required. I always like services that don't make you register. As I've said before, I have commitment issues.

 **Doomi** (doominow.com): A to-do list built with Adobe Air, which I find a cool platform. Offline and online synchronization.

 **Gubb** (gubb.net): Color code lists that are available via phone, e-mail and Web; they're prioritizable. You can share your lists and collaborate with others. And, according to gubb, they look good in print.

☑ **PRIVACY CHECK:** Gubb gets its money off of advertising, and it'll use your location and the information it gathers to show you targeted ads. They state, "We provide advertisers only aggregated non-personal information such as the number of times one of their ads was clicked. We do not sell, rent or otherwise share your personal information with any third parties except in the limited circumstances described in our Privacy Policy, such as when we believe we are required to do so by law."

 **Teuxdeux** (teuxdeux.com): Simple but attractive and easy-to-use to-do list with a nice week overview. Free with iPhone app.

 **Things** (culturedcode.com/things): Mac-based tool with an iPhone app. It's on the high end of a low-cost tool, but it's won all kind of awards and worth a look. $49.95 for single user, $74.95 for family pack. iPhone app is $9.99.

 **Toodledo** (www.toodledo.com): All kinds of little folders, subtasks due dates, tags, time estimates to make your task lists detail-icious. Free tool with a $2.99 iPhone and iPad app.

133

Dial2Do

www.dial2do.com

NO MORE TEXTING AND DRIVING

With the recent demise of Jott, one of my all-time favorite tools, the next best thing to keep you from texting while driving is Dial2Do. Sure, you have to pay $5.99 a month for that, but if you go Pro you can also send, listen and reply to e-mail, send and listen to tweets, and record notes to Evernote. Plus, it also integrates with Google Calendar, Xpenser, Remember the Milk, ToodleDo, Tumblr, and Wordpress.

And there must be a lot of people missing Jott these days as Dial2Do has a special just for people who used to use that service.

SMARTPHONE APPS: Android and Blackberry

134

Soshiku

soshiku.com

FREE

For the basic plan. Pro is $5 a month.

REMINDERS AND PROJECT MANAGEMENT FOR STUDENTS

My assistant, Claire, is a student, and she was particularly enamored with this tool. Soshiku manages high school or college assignments, keeping track of what's due and when and notifying you via e-mail or SMS.

One of the things Claire loved about it was its ability to coordinate with other students on group projects. Soshiku keeps track of when your assignments are due and can even notify you via e-mail or SMS. If a student has a big assignment with partners, they can chat online, collaborate with notes, share tasks and exchange files.

Founder Andrew Schaper told me the name Soshiku comes from the Japanese verb "soshiki suru," which means "to organize." Andrew said, "As a student, I wanted a reliable way to keep track of my schoolwork online and on my phone, but there weren't any services available that served those needs."

Right now Soshiku primarily targets students, but they're looking to expand the functionality to integrate teachers' needs and school-wide integration.

SMARTPHONE APPS: Palm Pre

135

Task.fm

task.fm

FREE

For the basic level, and the Pro is less than $4 a month.

 FREE SMS AND E-MAIL REMINDERS

The Web is now full of helpful reminder systems. I like Task.fm because you can write the way you speak and it converts your note into a smart reminder, such as if you tell it to remind you about "my meeting with Scott Thursday at noon." You can set reminders to come to you via text, e-mail, Twitter or a phone call.

ALSO CHECK OUT

 **Email Future** (emailfuture.com): E-mail yourself reminders on important dates such as anniversaries, birthdays or the opening day anniversary of your favorite bakery, when they sell cupcakes at retro prices. Founder Mike Rogers tells me, "Also, people really like to send themselves time capsule e-mails such as 'in 10 years, you better be married, rich, famous and working for Company XYZ.'"

 **Hit Me Later** (www.hitmelater.com): When you're too busy to respond to an e-mail right away, just forward it to 24@hitmelater.com, and Hit Me Later will resend it to you 24 hours later. Or send it to yourself in 4 hours with 4@hitmelater.com or next week with Tuesday@hitmelater.com. Anything under 24 hours is free, within the month is $12 a year and within the year is $30 a year.

136

JUST 'CUZ YOU CAN

 Remember those phone trees from your Girl Scout days? One mom would call two moms, then those moms each had two to call, etc. These days many of us rely on text messages or e-mails to disseminate messages to several people quickly, but sometimes a voicemail blast is the way to go. Sign up for a free account at **Phonevite** (www.phonevite.com), and you can send a voice message to 25 calls at once. Great for updating meeting times, canvassing for a volunteer or getting out a message on the go. Have a bigger network? The Premium level costs just a nickel per completed call.

Wakerupper

wakerupper.com

 FREE REMINDER AND WAKE-UP CALLS

Schedule a call with Wakerupper (try saying it aloud – Wake-ER-upper? Wake-Rupper?), and receive reminders via phone. You can even type a short message for your reminder call. All free. A premium service gives you snooze options and recurring call service for a nickel a call. Cool!

☑ **PRIVACY CHECK:** The free version of Wakerupper will show you targeted ads based on your location, call history and other info. They do not rent, sell or share your personal info with others. They store your telephone alerts, contact lists and other info as needed.

Google Calendar

www.google.com/calendar

FREE

 INTEGRATE ALL YOUR CALENDARS INTO ONE

One of my readers contributed Google Calendar as an organizing tool as a way to synchronize tasks and events:

"I was constantly trying to reconcile calendars: my work calendar from Lotus Notes, my partner's calendar from Outlook, event calendars, team calendars. It was a huge manual effort. Google Calendar can import from almost any source, share information with others, sync with your smartphone. It's quite possibly the best, most flexible calendaring tool available."

Many of my favorite tools integrate with Google Calendar, including Remember the Milk (page 132) and more. It doesn't have smartphone applications per se, but their mobile site is designed to be especially smartphone friendly.

139

13

Office Suites and Other Software Packages

Remember when open source applications became all the rage ten years ago, so free and low-cost software popped up all over the place?

Whole communities came together to write code for software that would compete with Microsoft Office and some of the other mega-companies that had a lock on some of the best applications in the marketplace.

The revolution proved a huge benefit for consumers – techies and non-techies alike. One of the best developments was the creation of rival suites of software that can bring together groups into a common platform for easier (and less expensive) collaboration.

This chapter covers several suites that offer an amazing array of tools. Many of these tools belong in different chapters of the book, so be sure to peruse the suites to find the best tools to meet your needs.

IN THIS CHAPTER:

13 · Office Suites and Other Software Packages

OpenOffice.org

www.openoffice.org

FREE

OpenOffice.org is 100 percent free.

 **A FULL-SERVICE SUITE OF TOOLS**

One of the first pioneers into the Office-knockoff market was OpenOffice.org, first released in 2002. OpenOffice.org was from the outset a suite of tools designed to interact with each other and encourage online collaboration. The site recorded more than 100 million downloads of the previous version in one year, and the latest version, OpenOffice.org 3.2, plays nice on almost all platforms: Windows, Mac, Linux and more. The suite has always been able to open similar documents from other software (such as MS Office documents), and the latest version creates files that MS Office 2007 will open.

Download the whole suite with a click, and all the applications are installed at once. OpenOffice.org doesn't allow online collaboration, but it's easy to send documents back and forth as attachments. Since OpenOffice.org can open documents from other software and can save in different formats, groups with different software packages can collaborate easily with OpenOffice.org in the mix.

The OpenOffice.org application names do what they say and say what they do:

➡ **Writer:** Word Processor

➡ **Calc:** Spreadsheet Software

➡ **Impress:** Presentation Software

➡ **Draw:** Graphics Editing

➡ **Base:** Database Creation

142

Its cousin, **StarOffice** (bit.ly/U2Fstaroffice), offers a bit more functionality, a touch more compatibility and a smidge more professionalism – for about fifty bucks.

ALSO CHECK OUT

 **NeoOffice.org** (www.neooffice.org): The free version of OpenOffice for Mac.

Zoho

www.zoho.com

FREE

Free for personal use.

 THERE'S AN APP FOR *EVERYTHING*!

Another company, Zoho, went a little nuts with its suite of software. It's amazing! The applications are all integrated and all online, though there are a few downloadable gadgets and widgets and plug-ins to make Zoho an even bigger part of your life. Most of the personal editions of the Zoho applications are free, and the business/enterprise versions (when you have more stuff to do) fall into the bargain category.

- ➡ **Zoho Mail:** Web-based e-mail service

- ➡ **Zoho CRM:** On-demand CRM solution

- ➡ **Zoho Writer:** Online word processor

- ➡ **Zoho Discussions:** Customer support forums and intranet

- ➡ **Zoho Sheet:** Online spreadsheets

- ➡ **Zoho Assist:** On-demand remote support

- ➡ **Zoho Show:** Online presentation

- ➡ **Zoho Creator:** Platform to create database apps

- ➡ **Zoho Docs:** Online document management

- ➡ **Zoho Invoice:** Online invoicing

- ➡ **Zoho Notebook:** Online note taker

- ➡ **Zoho Meeting:** Web conferencing, online meeting

- ➡ **Zoho Wiki:** Free online collaboration

144

- ➡ **Zoho Projects:** Project management software

- ➡ **Zoho Share:** Centralized public repository

- ➡ **Zoho Planner:** Online organizer

- ➡ **Zoho Recruit:** Applicant tracking system

- ➡ **Zoho Chat:** Online group chat

- ➡ **Zoho People:** Online HRIS

- ➡ **Zoho Business:** E-mail hosting and office suite

And on it goes ...

ALSO CHECK OUT

 **SourceForge** (www.sourceforge.net): A tremendous repository of open source software. "For the most part, everything is FREE!" said reader Dan Kelsey of the Indiana State Medical Association. He uses SourceForge to find applications and templates for both home and work.

Google Apps

www.google.com/apps

 100% APT APPS

Google jumped into the free application game in a big way a little later than most. The cool thing about the Google products is that they integrate with both each other and a host of other technologies. Everything is stored online, so this free service also includes free virtual hard drives.

Associations, nonprofits and academic professionals can take advantage of either discounted pricing for the Google Apps Premiere Edition or a completely free version with the Google Apps Education Edition. Both provide more security, more access, more storage and better support.

➡ **Gmail:** Webmail service

➡ **Google Calendar:** Calendaring service

➡ **Google Talk:** Instant messaging service

➡ **Google Docs:** Suite of products including word processers, spreadsheets, presentation tools

➡ **Google Sites Web Application:** Coding-free web pages for intranets and team-managed sites

➡ **Google Video:** Private, secure, hosted video sharing

➡ **Google Contacts:** Personal and shared contact lists

➡ **Google Groups:** Discussion groups

146

ALSO CHECK OUT

 **Google Wave** (www.wave.google.com): This looked literally like it was going to be the wave of the future. The experimental system put the functionality of many of these free and low-cost tools into one interface, grouped together and integrated with people in your work and life circles.

The system let you install integrations for all kinds of tools, such as those that help you plan meetings (like the tools that start on page 46), collaborate on documents, doodle together (see Dabbleboard, page 194) and much, much more. Collaboration was in real time – I mean really, real time. You could see people typing their responses to you.

CHEAP TIP:
Bringing the free tools together.

But apparently this kind of full control into our daily computer lives was a little too much for most users. Google pulled the plug on Wave in August 2010 because adoption was slow. The cool thing is that the technology behind Wave still exists, and we can expect the future to bring more integration and technology saturation, linking together more tools and making our lives easier.

147

Office Web Apps

office.microsoft.com/en-us/web-apps/

 TOTALLY SUITE APPS

Now that the competition in the office suite software area has gotten so fierce, Microsoft is starting to create free applications as well. The new online suite, Office Web Apps, runs through Windows Live, which currently offers SkyDrive (page 155), a document storage and sharing system, as well as Live Mesh (page 151), which stores documents online, synchronizes them among computers and permits remote access to computers. The Office Web Apps include Office-lite versions of Word, Excel, OneNote and PowerPoint, and, like Google Apps, allow real-time collaboration and editing.

Whatever office suite you plan on using, count on seeing a larger variety of suites from people you work with, and plenty more real-time collaboration and online document storage from everyone. And with those scenarios, be prepared for increased discussions about security, privacy and the need for redundant storage capabilities. The more we share our favorite toys, the more we'll have to deal with people who don't play well with others.

14

Back-Up Tools and Online Hosting

Isn't storing everything on your own hard drive so 2008?

These days many of these free and low-cost resources make use of cloud computing, where shared resources, software and information are hosted "out there somewhere" on the Web, and we access them from any computer (or perhaps smartphone) when we need them.

Cloud computing has tremendous advantages and worrisome disadvantages. I love knowing I can reach my work files from anyone's computer, and it's great feeling confident that all my projects are backed up and synchronized across all my computers.

But I'm taking a risk. I once ran a wonderful writing community's blog in Philadelphia, and when the no-name little hosting company we used had a computer meltdown, we lost everything.

Poof. Gone.

Can that happen to my files in the cloud? Of course. But it's a risk I'm willing to take, and something I plan for. If one of the services that I use online disappears, I know that I have my most important files on my laptop, a copy on my desktop and a full set of the data secure with my online backup service.

This chapter focuses on a number of cloud computing companies that help you store your files online, synchronize them among your computers, back them up and share them with others.

IN THIS CHAPTER:

| Dropbox
www.dropbox.com | **FREE**
For the basic plan. Pro is
$5 a month. |

 STORE, SHARE AND SYNC YOUR FILES

One of the most popular of the cloud computing tools is Dropbox, a great little service my readers have mentioned several times since it was founded in 2007.

Dropbox allows you to synchronize your files among your computers and also stores them online for access anywhere. This is a fantastic application for those of us who travel and don't want to deal with throwing files on thumb drives. Its storage capacity matches Mozy.com (page 155) for backups and its feature set is on par with Live Mesh, my personal favorite (see below).

As one reader wrote, "It works great, and it's free. Very comforting to know my files are backed up offsite. They are also available by logging into Dropbox, so you have access to them from anywhere." And Dr. Alan Greene from DrGreene.com says he uses Dropbox on his iPhone to have access to all his files on the road.

SMARTPHONE APPS: iPhone

151

ALSO CHECK OUT

 **Box.net** (www.box.net): 1GB is free with personal accounts, but business accounts graduate into file storage plus project management (and the price goes up to $15 per user per month). Gwen Goldfarb of the Goldfarb Group (an association management company) says she uses Box.net to share documents and collaborate with her association members.

 **Live Mesh** (www.mesh.com): Microsoft's version and my favorite. Up to 5GB free.

 **Nomadesk** (www.nomadesk.com): The name is a marriage of "nomad" and "desk." $50 a year for sharing for up to 3 computers and unlimited file storage. $15 a month for lots more features, including a nifty way to e-mail your files to the online fileserver.

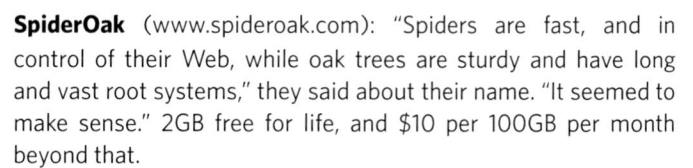 **OpenDrive** (www.opendrive.com): The free level puts a watermark on files and doesn't include synchronization, but it's only $4.99 a month for more features and up to 100GB.

SpiderOak (www.spideroak.com): "Spiders are fast, and in control of their Web, while oak trees are sturdy and have long and vast root systems," they said about their name. "It seemed to make sense." 2GB free for life, and $10 per 100GB per month beyond that.

 **Syncplicity** (www.syncplicity.com): 2GB free, $15 for up to 50GB.

CHEAP CASE STUDY	**Cloud computing on the fly**
	Beth Ziesenis

When I'm on the road, I depend on these types of synchronization tools more than the application on my iPhone that tells me where to find the nearest cupcake (that'd be Layar, page 215).

You create an account and add computers to your network. When I work on my desktop computer in the office, any file in my shared folders is updated on the Live Mesh site. When I sign onto my laptop computer, the files are automatically updated. When I'm working on a plane (one of the old-fashioned kinds without wi-fi), I can modify the files, and as soon as I connect to the Internet again, all the files are updated on all the connected computers.

Live Mesh also lets you remotely access computers in your mesh, but this service doesn't seem as robust as LogMeIn (page 24).

Screencast.com

www.screencast.com

FREE

Up to 2GB of storage space and 2GB of bandwidth for views.

 YOUR OWN ONLINE LIBRARY

I adore Screencast.com. This service lets you upload and share documents, Jing captures (page 66), video files, etc. into a library of your own. One of my favorite features is the playlist. When I give feedback on a client's document, sometimes I'll capture several screenshots. Then I put all the screenshots into a playlist and send the client one link to review.

I had to buy a one-time upgrade for 100GB of bandwidth per month since my account gets lots of traffic when I put a Screencast.com capture on my blog. A Pro account gives you 25GB of storage and up to 200GB of bandwidth monthly for $9.99 a month.

☑ **PRIVACY CHECK:** Screencast.com uses cookies to gauge page popularity and analyze site traffic. They collect your e-mail address when you register, and people with whom you share your media can contact you through Screencast.com. Your e-mail address is never visible. Screencast.com will e-mail you with news about updates, promotions and surveys, but you can opt out. The policy of TechSmith, the parent company, is to never rent, share or sell your information with others.

153

ALSO CHECK OUT

 **SoundCloud** (www.soundcloud.com): Specializes in storing and moving music files.

 **FileDropper** (www.filedropper.com): Easy as anything ... just upload your file and get a link to send. Period.

ContactOffice

www.contactoffice.com

FREE

At most basic level.

 YOUR INBOX WHEN YOU'RE OUT AND ABOUT

ContactOffice puts your e-mails, contacts, schedule, tasks and documents into a virtual office environment. It really has a little bit of everything, from polling to sending text messages to live chat and group collaboration. Play around with the demo on their site for a few minutes to understand the full scope of the many components that work together. It's quite a package.

The European-based company has been around since 1999 and includes multiple language platforms to help bring together an international team. Plus, it has a tool to sync with the data on several smartphones, including iPhone, BlackBerry and more. These aren't smartphone apps, but it does allow you to add any calendar items from your phone to your ContactOffice desktop. And you can get to your ContactOffice site on any phone that surfs the Web.

Their pricing gets a little confusing but in order to use some of the cool group features, someone in the group has to pay monthly fees at the appropriate levels.

Mozy Online Backup

www.mozy.com

AUTOMATED ONLINE BACKUP

Mozy was one of the first online backup services I discovered, and my readers keep telling me it's their favorite. You just set up a Mozy account; tell it which drives, folders and files to back up; and let it get to work. It can work in the background all the time or back up on a schedule. If your computer blows up, you can restore your files to another machine, and it also keeps 30-days of versions of your past files, just in case you need to recover an earlier version of a document (ever hit "Save" instead of "Save As …"?)

ALSO CHECK OUT

Carbonite (www.carbonite.com): Unlimited storage for $54.95 a year.

ADrive (www.adrive.com): 50GB of storage free! Yes, 50! $6.95 a month gives you that same 50 GB with many more benefits.

Windows SkyDrive (login.live.com): Free backup for up to 25GB, but you have to add one file at a time.

Wuala (www.wuala.com): Think "voilà," the French word for, umm … voilà. 1GB free, and packages starting at $29 for various size plans.

155

Backupify

www.backupify.com

 BACKUP SOLUTION FOR ONLINE DATA SUCH AS GMAIL, FACEBOOK, TWITTER, BASECAMP, FLICKR, ETC.

Are your tweets and Facebook postings works of art? Backupify can help you preserve them forever so your kids and grandkids have a permanent record of what you ate for breakfast every day and your reviews of local cupcake shops.

All kidding aside, preserving your online data from services such as Gmail, Flickr, Basecamp (page 123) and social networks can protect you from hackers, prevent loss of valuable data and perhaps keep you in compliance if you are required to keep records of your online data for legal reasons.

The company tells me that a favorite feature is Backupify's ability to produce a PDF of all your tweets.

156

15

Taking Care of You

Do you spend too much time sitting in front of a computer?

We all know we're supposed to stand up and stretch, sit up straight in the chair, position our wrists correctly and all that stuff. But do we do it? Sometimes we need a little help, a few reminders to keep us focused on the little things we can do to take care of ourselves at the computer and beyond.

Here are a handful of resources that can keep your work day more productive, your body less strained and your eyes more relaxed.

IN THIS CHAPTER:

ErgonomicsSimplified

www.ergonomicssimplified.com

FREE

Up to 2GB, and up to 20GB
is $4.99 a year.

A FREE EVALUATION TOOL TO EXAMINE YOUR WORK ENVIRONMENT

This site takes you through a series of questions about your chair position, your mouse, your monitor height and more. The evaluation gives you tips as you answer the questions, and at the end you get a full list of problem areas and recommendations for products (which they sell.) But the free quiz is well worth a few minutes.

ErgonomicsSimplified President Chris Sorrells says a professional evaluation from an ergonomics consultant may cost close to $350, so this tool can save you money and perhaps give you recommendations to make your life in the chair a little more comfy. What did I learn? The chair I bought at a garage sale is too short. The desk my husband gave me is too tall. My monitors need to be elevated, and I should take more breaks.

And if I read between the lines of the report, I'm pretty sure they recommended more cupcakes for stress relief.

ALSO CHECK OUT

Big Stretch (www.monkeymatt.com/bigstretch): Automated reminders to keep you from spending too much time in front of the screen (download for Windows only).

BreatheText (www.breathetext.com): All together now ... Breathe! BreatheText sends out Twitter (page 219) messages when it's time for a cleansing breath.

Grooveshark

listen.grooveshark.com

FREE

*Free with ads, $6 a month
for added features.*

 MATCH YOUR MUSIC TO YOUR MOOD

Brian Carter (briancarteryeah.com) calls himself "the most hilarious search/social-department-directing, Miata-driving keynote speaker to ever make fun of Beth." He posed the burning question, "How can you work without music?" Brian recommended Grooveshark, an online music streaming company. Enter an artist or song you like, and Grooveshark will create a personal playlist to match your style.

ALSO CHECK OUT

 **Pandora** (www.pandora.com): This one's my favorite on both my computer and iPhone. The account is online, so I can get my stations on both.

159

F.lux

www.stereopsis.com/flux

FREE

 ADJUST THE LIGHTING ON YOUR COMPUTER SCREEN

My wonderful assistant, Claire, contributed this tool. F.lux adapts the lighting level of your computer's display to the time of day: warm at night and like sunlight during the day. F.lux makes your computer screen look like the room you're in, all the time. When the sun sets, it makes your computer look like your indoor lights. In the morning, it makes your screen look like sunlight again.

☑ **PRIVACY CHECK:** There is no privacy policy on their page or on the site for Cyberverse.com, the company that provides F.lux. The user agreement in the download does not contain information either.

160

Google Health
health.google.com

FREE

 TAKE CHARGE OF YOUR HEALTH

Google Health is one of those philanthropic tools that big companies share to show how wonderful they are. And it is wonderful. It helps you organize, manage and share your personal medical history to help you get a better picture of your health status. You can input your own stats, as well as download data from hospitals, doctors and pharmacies. It also integrates with other health tools, such as my favorite calorie tracker at **Livestrong.com**, allowing you to track weight loss goals and other health ideals.

In addition, you can use Google Health to track health habits directly, such as monitoring how much water you drink or how many cups of coffee you consume. I haven't seen a place to track cupcakes, but I'm sure it's an add-on somewhere.

Google Health is free for all, and you already have an account if you use Gmail or any other Google app.

161

16

IT Tools

Have you ever contemplated dating an IT guy just to have someone to call when your computer is ailing?

Personally? Yes … but my husband might take exception to that, so I'm very grateful for the tools in this chapter that help keep my computer up to date and running properly.

These tools bring expertise you never thought you had to your own machine. Some of the tools, like my favorite, CrossLoop (page 163), give you direct access to experts, while others put the tools for computer maintenance in your own hands, like FileHippo (page 164).

IN THIS CHAPTER:

CrossLoop

www.crossloop.com

YOUR OWN IT DEPARTMENT AT THE READY

CrossLoop is a network of IT specialists who are standing by to help you. Seriously. All you do is create an account, search for technicians who have experience with your type of computer issue, and let them take over your screen to fix the problem. A little icon tells you which technicians are actually online for immediate help. You pay their hourly rate (which varies by technician), and you can get first-rate advice without having to take them to dinner.

They've won *LAPTOP Magazine*'s Award for Innovation, plus they're a Windows 7 Editor's Pick and a CNET Download.com Top 5.

CHEAP TIP:

No matter how horrible your computer problem is, someone else has had it before. Copy and paste the error messages you get into Google, and you'll probably find forums where people have posted and solved the same issue.

163

ALSO CHECK OUT

Twelpforce (twitter.com/TWELPFORCE): Send an emergency tweet on Twitter to Twelpforce, the tech team from Best Buy, and they'll tweet you back ideas to fix your tech problems. Worked like a charm when my iPhone e-mail went haywire. Twelpforce gurus actually researched my host's site to discover their fix for the problem.

Zolved (www.zolved.com): Computer gurus hang out here to answer questions you never knew you had. Search the database or ask a guru for free. You can also phone a friend and ask him to dial into your computer remotely with Zolved's screensharing tool.

FileHippo.com Update Checker

FREE

www.filehippo.com

 QUICKLY DISCOVER OUTDATED
SOFTWARE ON YOUR MACHINE

If you're a free software fan, chances are your computer is full of ever-evolving applications that need regular updates. Use FileHippo.com's Update Checker to scan your machine. In minutes, you'll have a list of applications that need updates, along with the links to do so.

☑ **PRIVACY CHECK:** On the main page, they write, "The Update Checker will not send any personal information back to FileHippo.com. The only information collected is a list of programs and their versions, along with the operating system details to help with processing. Additionally none of this is linked to your IP address and the logs are deleted after processing."

164

Ninite

ninite.com

FREE

For personal us, $20 a month for professional.

A SUPER-COOL WAY TO DOWNLOAD COMMON FREE PROGRAMS

Oh, I love free stuff, and I love people who make it easier to download free stuff. Visit the Ninite site, and check off the free applications you want on your computer, such as Firefox, Chrome, iTunes, Audacity, Skype, AVG, Adobe Reader, GIMP ... The list is fantastic!

Once you choose your programs, click to install, and Ninite will manage your installation. This is great when you are doing a full upgrade to Windows 7 or setting up a new computer, like I had to do last spring. Discover a download in this book that's not on the list? Send them a note, and they'll consider adding it to their collection.

A note from the Ninite folks:

Ninite says "no" to any toolbars or other junk that come with apps. Ninite automatically selects the best version of an app based on your PC's language and 64-bit capabilities.

Platforms: Windows

JUST 'CUZ YOU CAN

Ever need to write a note you really, really don't want to let anyone keep around? Write your note through **Privnote** (privnote.com) to get a link to your message, and the message will disappear after the person reads it. It is the closest most of us will come to being James Bond.

165

TuneUp Utilities

www.tune-up.com

PRICE

$49.95 for use on up to three PCs.

 INCREASE YOUR PC'S PERFORMANCE

TuneUp Utilities keeps Windows clean and tunes up your PC to improve your computer's performance. With a one-click interface for many processes, you can defragment hard drives, clean up the registry and free up disk space. It also helps customize your Windows experience and offers up advice for fine tuning your system.

Platforms: Windows

166

OmniDiskSweeper

www.omnigroup.com/products/omnidisksweeper

FREE

 SCAN YOUR MAC FOR BLOATED FILES

OmniDiskSweeper is a Mac tool that quickly finds and deletes large files to make room on your hard drive. OmniDiskSweeper scans your disks, highlights the biggest files and notes which files are used by the system so you don't accidentally delete anything important. It's a fast, easy way to find everything that's hogging your drive and clear it out, so you've got room for the stuff you really need.

Platforms: Mac

17
Security Tools

How can we know who's lurking out there?

Keeping your computer protected against the bad guys who spam, steal and infect is a full-time job, and it's not an area where you should scrimp. Luckily, even this category has free and low-cost tools to help.

This chapter covers everything from anti-virus security suites to little tools that allow you to register safely and distribute your e-mail address without fear of spam. In addition, this chapter includes reader favorite RoboForm (page 174), which not only helps you create unique passwords but also saves you time in filling out forms.

IN THIS CHAPTER:

AVG Anti-Virus

www.free.avg.com

FREE ANTI-VIRUS SOFTWARE FOR PCS

AVG Stands for Anti-Virus Guard, and this award-winning company has been protecting PCs from viruses, spyware and other nasties since 2001.

Consultant Susan Klein loves it and uses it for her firewall and Internet security: "I use it in place of Norton and other security software. I've heard that computer gurus use it because it doesn't take up as much space as the security software you buy."

Bonus product: The AVG LinkScanner tool gives real-time protection from Web threats. The Search-Shield scans search results and places a safety rating next to each link, so you know where it's safe to click. The AVG folks said, "Online criminals are getting smarter. But we're always ahead of them. Our real-time AVG LinkScanner software detects threats at the only time it matters – before you arrive."

Platforms: Windows and Linux

169

ALSO CHECK OUT

avast! (www.avast.com): Free version gives basic protection, and $34.95 provides the Pro version for a year to one computer.

Spybot Search and Destroy (www.safer-networking.org): A fantastic, free utility that monitors your computer to protect against spyware.

CHEAP CASE STUDY	Beth Ziesenis
	When bad apps happen to good people

In an attempt to cut out distractions from my work day, I went on the hunt for a tool that would help me block out time-wasting sites such as Facebook and Twitter. I found success with K9 (page 19), but not before I embarked on a nightmare with a malicious free tool.

In 2008 I discovered a handy little computer babysitter that promised to help you "regain the productivity currently lost due to employees frivolous and inappropriate online chatting or non-business related surfing and shopping. I downloaded the free trial. More than two years later, I finally put down the computer that bore the brunt of the tool's havoc.

After the initial install, I didn't get a setup wizard which would have let me establish an admin password. As soon as I installed it, I saw it was a little rinky-dink program with bugs and a not-too-professional appearance. I tried to uninstall. It said, please disable the program first. I tried to disable. It said, "Please enter the admin password." THERE IS NO ADMIN PASSWORD.

This program was designed to be completely unremovable by naughty employees who don't want corporate big brother software on their personal machines. I downloaded uninstallers, consulted technology experts on my favorite listserv, tried to revert using Windows System Restore, left three messages with Zihtec's help desk (no response) ... I actually was able to remove most of it, but a little remnant remained. And the kicker – the remnant blocked some of my other programs and prevented me from being able to use Windows Task Manager to stop cranky programs. It even broke my Jing (page 66)!

I even consulted with experts on CrossLoop (page 163), to no avail. I spent days rebooting, downloading utilities, consulting with experts, cursing and finally came to the conclusion (with the experts) that I'd have to reformat my computer, wipe everything off and rebuild it. I put that step off as long as I could, and the machine finally ground to a halt this spring. Rest in peace.

In the autopsy, my computer consultant ran a malware scare of the old machine, and the presence of Internet Control for Business gave my machine a "High Risk" rating.

Immunet

www.immunet.com

FREE

Immunet Protect Free is free, and the Protect Plus version is $19.95.

VIRUS PROTECTION FROM THE MASSES

This is a clever idea. Immunet is a free anti-virus solution that uses the concept of cloud computing to set up a system that helps people work together to protect members against millions of online threats.

I'll let the creators of Immunet explain:

The idea behind Immunet is that it is a collective community where each member who is protected helps strengthen the immune system of the entire network of users. Each time a virus is detected on one computer within the Immunet Protection Network, ALL users are immediately protected from that very same virus, thus the concept of Collective Immunity which is unique to Immunet.

Immunet Protect works alongside all other traditional anti-virus products as an added layer of real-time protection that also protects your community.

Platforms: Windows

ALSO CHECK OUT

WinPatrol (www.winpatrol.com): Stops trojans before they install themselves into your Windows startup folder. Free for basic features or $30 for an upgrade.

171

Scr.im

scr.im

CONVERT YOUR E-MAIL TO A URL

Scr.im converts your e-mail address into a simple URL, and people who want to write you have to pass a simple test to show they're human. It's great for sharing addresses online, such as with Twitter, craigslist, Facebook and more.

172

10 Minute Mail

10minutemail.com

FREE

 EASY, SECURE, TEMPORARY E-MAIL TO PROTECT YOUR-SELF FROM UNSCRUPULOUS FREE SOFTWARE CREATORS

I hate to admit it, but even I've been duped into registering with a company that sells my e-mail address. That's why I love services like 10 Minute Mail, which gives you a temporary e-mail address to use for your registration.

Just go to the site for an address, use it to register, then return to 10 Minute Mail if you need to click on an additional link to complete the registration. Your e-mail will be good for a few minutes or a little longer if you need it.

173

RoboForm

www.roboform.com

 NEVER LOSE A PASSWORD AGAIN

PCWorld named RoboForm one of the 25 programs they never want to live without. Founded in 2000, RoboForm is a password manager and form filler-outer. It remembers your key information so you don't have to fill in long registration and checkout forms, and it logs you into your regular websites automatically. It can also help you generate secure passwords (something beyond Password1234) and keep secure notes.

Readers like Danny Brown, branding and emerging media consultant at dannybrown.me, love RoboForm:

"It allows me to have a different password for every online tool I use, and not have to remember it. Not only that, but it fills in your details for any registration pages – a definite bonus."

SMARTPHONE APPS:

➡ iPhone

➡ BlackBerry

➡ Palm Pre

➡ Android

18

PDF and File Conversion Tools

Do you PDF?

Adobe created the Portable Document Format (PDF) around 1993 and, in 2008, the .PDF file extension became an industry standard, no longer simply belonging to Adobe software. For many years now we know that "just send me a PDF" means "throw it to me in a good-looking format so that I can open it without it looking messed up on my computer."

Many tools these days can help you create, manage and manipulate PDFs, which are designed to be a little inflexible without the premium software. These free and low-cost tools are meant to cobble together most of the features of Adobe Acrobat Pro, more or less. In addition, free tools abound to help you convert and open mystery files with extensions you've never heard of.

175

IN THIS CHAPTER:

Adobe Acrobat Pro www.adobe.com	**$449** *For full version, or upgrade* *from $159.*

 THE ULTIMATE PDF TOOL

Before I get into all the ways that you can get around not having Adobe Acrobat Professional, let me point out that the very expensive software inevitably shows up on any poll I do about software that's worth the price. Adobe sells the full version for $449 (Mac or Windows), and if you find yourself creating, editing or cussing at PDFs on a regular basis, you might find buying the software is worth your time.

Adobe Acrobat Pro lets you convert almost any file into a PDF, merge multiple documents into one PDF and maintain converted multimedia.

You can also password-protect files and set permissions. You can invite a team to comment on a PDF, and Acrobat also helps you create fillable forms for gathering data, which you can then export and view in a spreadsheet.

"Although there is a price tag, this has saved me so much time and effort that it is well worth the price," said longtime reader Carol Watkins, certified association executive (CAE), from the National Dental EDI Council.

There you have it.

Bonus! **ADOBE READER** (free) now includes highlighting and commenting capabilities and was a huge help in working on the final drafts of the book!

177

Convert PDF to Word

www.convertPDFtoword.net

FREE

 PDF QUICK CONVERSION SITE

This strange little site does all kinds of handy things. Convert PDF to Word does just what it says. Easily. And free. Just upload your PDF, and in a few minutes, download the Word doc. Can't get much better.

Oh wait, yes it can ... look across the top of the page, and you'll see their other conversion sites:

➡ **Convert PDF to text** (www.convertPDFtotext.net)

➡ **Convert PDF to image** (www.convertPDFtoimage.com)

➡ **Convert PDF to HTML** (www.convertPDFtohtml.net)

➡ **Convert text to PDF** (www.texttoPDFconverter.com)

➡ **Convert Word to PDF** (www.convertword2PDF.com)

☑ **PRIVACY CHECK:** This one is a mystery. No contact info and no privacy policy. I've used the service several times with zero issues, and my train wreck of a computer (now deceased) was just analyzed for malware, and this never came up. The site is full of Google ads and other sponsors, including DocQ (page 180). I spoke to DocQ, and even they didn't know who ran it, but they trust it enough to advertise there.

ALSO CHECK OUT

 **PDF2Word** (www.PDFonline.com/PDF2word/index.asp): Same concept, and they also have a downloadable converter for $19.95. Reader Betty Kjellberg (www.fabricofcollaboration.com) said the site has been a reliable help for her in working with clients.

Nitro PDF Free Suite

www.nitroPDF.com/free/index.htm

 A HOST OF FREE PDF TOOLS

Nitro PDF sells a competitor to Adobe Acrobat for $99, but it also has a whole host of free online and downloadable PDF toys. No registration required, no ads attached and their products regularly make the top download lists on CNET.

➡ **PDF to Word Converter** (www.PDFtoword.com): Downloadable and online.

➡ **PDF to Excel Converter** (www.PDFtoexcelonline.com): Also online and downloadable.

➡ **PrimoPDF** (www.primoPDF.com): Download the application to enable one-click PDF creation from almost any Windows application (300+ file types) and many more cool features.

➡ **PrimoOnline** (www.primoPDF.com/online.aspx): Online converter of 300+ file types.

➡ **PDF Download** (www.PDFdownload.org): Download a plug-in for your favorite browser to quickly save a page as a PDF, or enter the URL of a site into the online converter and let the system e-mail you the page as a PDF attachment.

➡ **PDF Hammer** (www.PDFhammer.com): Combine, rearrange and delete PDF pages.

Platforms: Windows

179

PDFescape

www.PDFescape.com

FREE

 THE PDF EDITOR I'VE BEEN DREAMING OF!

I'm often frustrated when my clients send me PDFs to edit because I have to do screenshots with Jing (page 66) page by page. Don't get me wrong – I adore Jing, but the process takes forever. But PDFescape lets you upload a PDF and add all the notes you need without having to have Adobe Acrobat.

ALSO CHECK OUT

 **PDFtypewriter** (www.ctdeveloping.com/ctdeveloping/products/PDFtypewriter_info.asp): From the same makers as PDFescape, PDFtypewriter is a downloadable PDF creator, editor and more for $29.99.

 **DocQ** (www.docq.com): A variety of free and paid PDF options with responsive and immediate customer service.

FillAnyPDF

www.FillAnyPDF.com

SEND LINKS TO A PDF FORM AND TRACK THE RESULTS

Upload a PDF form to FillAnyPDF.com and send out the links. Even if your PDF is not interactive, people can still fill it out so you can track the results.

Founder Brian Wiblan told me, "People always sent me PDF forms that weren't 'fillable,' so I had to print them to fill them out. I made the site because I wanted a way to fill them out and sign them online."

Upload and e-mail your form, and you can track who filled it out.

181

YouConvertIt

www.youconvertit.com

 QUICK FILE CONVERSION AND SHARING

YouConvertIt is an online file converter system that makes it easy for online users to convert their files without installing anything on their computers. YouConvertIt will also help you download YouTube videos and send large files via e-mail.

YouConvertIt automatically detects the format of your file and gives you options for possible conversions. *PC Magazine* called it one of the top websites of 2008.

They also give you free inbox space to manage and share your converted documents, plus have added an online backup tool (see chapter 14, page 149, for more backup tools).

ALSO CHECK OUT

 **Media Converter** (www.mediaconverter.org): A free Firefox plug-in to help you convert media files.

 **Zamzar** (www.zamzar.com): File converter and online storage. Basic level starts at $7 a month.

182

OpenWith

www.openwith.org

 FREE PROGRAMS TO OPEN ANY FILE EXTENSION

Ever get a document that your computer doesn't recognize and you have no idea where to look? OpenWith.org helps you identify any file extension and finds you a free program to open it. You can either search online for the right program or download the Desktop Tool (PC only).

As their site says:

"All of us at OpenWith.org have found ourselves helping our parents and friends open obscure file types time and time again, and decided that this information was best shared with everybody. There are plenty of great programs out there that will cost you hundreds of dollars to do what you need. What you probably don't know is that there is usually free software that is just as good. You just don't know about it."

Platforms: Windows

183

OCR Terminal

www.ocrterminal.com

 CONVERT PDF AND JPGS TO WORD

In my next life I want to come back as a programmer with a heart like these guys to create a tool that's so helpful. OCR Terminal solves a challenge I've had multiple times ... I receive a PDF that I need to edit in Word, or a graphic of text that I need to tweak.

Many free OCR (optical character recognition) software programs are less than precise, and I usually end up retyping the whole thing. Ugh. OCR Terminal lets you upload a PDF, JPG or other types of files and converts them instantly into editable, searchable text. I had a PDF of a magazine article I wrote, and in about 90 seconds I had the version in Word ... not quite perfect, but darn close.

It's cool because you can preserve the formatting and page layout so your tables, images, captions and headers don't go haywire in the new document.

Another cool thing: OCR Terminal can recognize and process 19 languages. And a desktop download lets you process several files at the same time. As OCR Terminal tells me, "So you can process 20 files waiting on your desktop, get some coffee and and come back to see all results automatically downloaded and waiting for you."

You can purchase more conversions per page ($.09 per page for up to 50 pages), with subscription models (starting at $10 a month for up to 150 pages) or in bulk (2,500 pages for $99). The desktop tool is in beta.

Platforms: Windows

19

Web Meetings, Webinars and Presentations

But what if we can't all be in the same room?

When you're working on projects with people from across the country or around the world, sometimes you literally need to be on the same page, looking at the same screen, talking about the same document and giving real-time feedback. Webinars have also become essential these days, as travel budgets have tightened and more people just don't have time to spend 3 days out of the office at a conference.

Screensharing software used to be very expensive, and only the biggest corporations could afford it. But these days there are a host of free and low-cost tools that allow you to send a link to 1 person or a thousand people to ask them to watch what's on your desktop, talk to you via phone or online and interact almost as if you were in the same conference room.

This chapter covers services that allow you to share your screen, as well as a few PowerPoint-type tools that let you create amazing presentations for live events or stand-alone viewings.

IN THIS CHAPTER:

GoToMeeting

www.gotomeeting.com

$49
Up to 15 attendees for $49 a month or $468 a year.

 A STANDARD IN LOW-COST SCREENSHARING

I consider GoToMeeting the company that put screensharing into the realm of possible for small companies with smaller budgets. They were the first company I discovered that offered affordable, do-it-yourself options for putting on webinars and working remotely with groups. I was a subscriber for about a year even when lower-cost options were available because the product was so solid and the features so robust.

The GoToWebinar package lets you put on as many webinars as you want with up to 1,000 people per session. You go through a step-by-step process to set it up, including creating an invitation e-mail, setting up poll questions, personalizing the waiting room that will show before the session starts and more. You can also invite presenters with separate e-mails, upload their bios and invite them to special practice sessions. I like that during the event participants can raise their virtual hands and ask questions via the chat window, and you can professionally hand off controls of the screen to other presenters.

After the webinar, you can send a survey, see reports on your attrition rate and how much people paid attention, plus you can download rosters. You can also make the archive of your meeting available. To me the whole experience of putting on a webinar with this service makes your outfit look professional and organized, and I thought it was worth $99 a month.

Use **GoToWebinar** with up to 1,000 attendees for $99 a month or $948 a year and **GoToTraining** with up to 200 trainees for $149 a month or $1428 a year.

join.me

join.me

 FREE WEBINARS FOR ALL

My friends at LogMeIn (page 24) have made me very happy. They created join. me, an instant screensharing tool. You don't even have to register to share your screen – just click the share button, download a little something-something and start sharing.

Join.me is perfect for low-cost webinars. You can invite up to 250 people to your event, and you can give screen control to another presenter. It includes a free conference call number and code, and you can also communicate through the interactive chat. It works on all common browsers and platforms.

For $29 a month or $299 a year you can personalize your own join.me link and set up webinars or meetings ahead of time.

Simple. Easy. Awesome.

ALSO CHECK OUT

 **Yugma** (www.yugma.com): This tool has a free version for 2 people. Their Pro version for up to 20 gives you lots more features for $9.95 a month.

Show Document

www.showdocument.com

INSTANT, EASY DESKTOP SHARING

Show Document lets you share a document, whiteboard, YouTube video – all kinds of stuff – with a very, very, very quick touch of a button. You can have up to 3 attendees for free, or unlimited for about 30 bucks a month. The upgrade allows you to integrate audio and video and gives you lots of other cool options.

☑ **PRIVACY CHECK:** The documents you upload will be permanently deleted after your session ends, and they will not share your personal information with a third party. They track non-personal information to analyze site traffic.

CHEAP CASE STUDY	**Running a small business with free and low-cost tools**
	Dallon Christensen

189

I converted to web-based technology in the fall of 2009 when my wife and I started keeping our checkbook register on a Google Docs spreadsheet (page 195). As soon as we started using Google, we loved being able to access and edit our register on any computer. When I started FirstStep Concepts in January 2010, I wanted to minimize my technology expenses. Using web-based tools was an easy decision after my experience with our checkbook register. We also have a laptop and a netbook at home, and using web-based software allows me to use either computer with no loss of productivity.

I start my day by scheduling informational tweets and LinkedIn updates with Hootsuite (page 219), a free social network organizer. Since I still work a full-time job, I use Hootsuite to space my tweets throughout the day. Hootsuite lets me maintain a regular Twitter (page 219) presence throughout the day, even though I am working. While I am at work, I use the Google Apps free version to check my work e-mail and combined calendar at lunch. I have used Gmail for my personal e-mail since 2007, and I love the ability to use e-mail tags instead of folders and to pull e-mails from multiple e-mail accounts into one location. I also show all of my calendars (personal, work and home/school) on my Google Apps calendar.

I maintain my business plan and financial forecasts with PlanHQ's planning software (page 106). PlanHQ allows me to track goals, develop action plans, and compare my actual vs. forecast financial results from any computer for $9/month.

I am currently testing FreshBooks (page 96) and LessAccounting (page 97) for my accounting software. My coaching practice has no inventory or assets except for my desk, computer and printer. Both of these programs allow me to invoice customers, record expenses and prepare financial statements much like a traditional accounting program would do. Both programs start with free versions, and I will increase features and cost as I grow my business. I can even brand my sites with my logo and colors. QuickBooks Online is also a good option to use for businesses with inventory. I use 37signals' Highrise program for my customer relationship management system. This program is also free until I have 250 clients.

I love working with Web-based software for many reasons. I worry less about my hard drive or flash drive crashing. I am paying for only the features I need and can easily upgrade when I need to do so. I keep my technology expenses under $30/month. Finally, I plan to convert from a PC to a Mac in the next year. Since I access my technology through the Internet, I foresee little to no trouble transferring my operations to a Mac laptop.

Dallon Christensen, creative director and founder of FirstStep Concepts, a business decisions coaching firm.

Prezi

www.prezi.com

 NOT YOUR AVERAGE POWERPOINT PRESENTATION

And now for something completely different. Think of Prezi as an endless whiteboard that you can use to tell a story. You put up images and words, and then you sweep a camera across the board, zooming in and out of points as you talk about them.

Instead of creating point-by-point slides, you illustrate your presentation with graphics, words and ideas. Then you use the tool to move from one point to the next, and the tool allows you to swirl in, pull out and do all kinds of special effects.

Association coaching professional Jon Hockman of The d3 Group (www.thed3group.com) said, "It's a WAY better way to tell a story than PowerPoint." As I've said before, I'm a pretty linear chick, and PowerPoints work just fine for me. But for people who are tired of the same old slide situations, Prezi may be just the ticket.

Education professionals can use the $59 level free.

191

SlideRocket

www.sliderocket.com

FREE

Basic level is free, and the professional versions start at $24 per month per user.

A WEB-BASED PRESENTATION TOOL
WITH SUPER-DUPER SPECIAL EFFECTS

SlideRocket is an online presentation platform that lets you create, manage, share and measure the impact of your presentations. Watch a few of the presentation demos, and you'll see a whole host of cool special effects, professional touches and entertaining multimedia.

It's easy to use, and all your presentations are accessible online, meaning you no longer have to worry about whether you have the full version of PowerPoint on your computer.

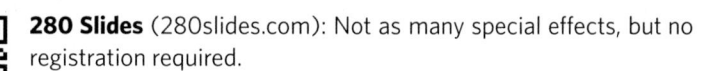

ALSO CHECK OUT

280 Slides (280slides.com): Not as many special effects, but no registration required.

WebSlides (slides.diigo.com): Turns your bookmarks and feeds into an interactive slideshow – a new way of organizing, sharing and presenting content you like from the Web.

SlideShare (www.slideshare.net): Bills itself as the world's largest community for sharing presentations. Things you can do with your presentations uploaded to Slideshare include public or private viewing settings, downloading presentations by others on any topic to reuse or remix and embedding on blogs, websites or company intranets.

JUST 'CUZ YOU CAN

 Mac users, this one's for you! I'm dying to try out **OmniDazzle** (www.omnigroup.com/products/omnidazzle), a free tool that adds special effects to presentations. Lucky Mac users can download the software to add cool ways to highlight screens, words and points during presentations. Oh how I wish we poor PC people had a similar version!

Dabbleboard

www.dabbleboard.com

FREE

For the basics, or starting at $8 a month if you want to be able to download, control and save your creations.

 EASY ONLINE WHITEBOARDING IN REAL TIME

Dabbleboard is another one of those instant tools that doesn't make you register, although if you do, you get access to more features. Simply push the "Get Started" button, and you have a whiteboard to work with. Draw pictures, import documents, invite friends. The canvas is yours. It was a *PC Magazine* Top 100 tool, and I like the feature that turns a freehand, misshapen, shaky circle into a real circle graphic.

Look for Dabbleboard to launch their new Web conference tool, **AlmostMeet**, and they plan to add other types of desktop sharing options.

ALSO CHECK OUT
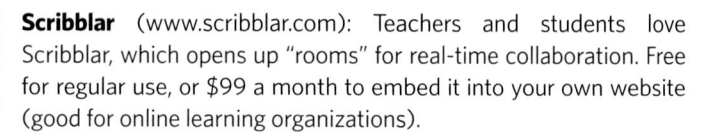

 **Scribblar** (www.scribblar.com): Teachers and students love Scribblar, which opens up "rooms" for real-time collaboration. Free for regular use, or $99 a month to embed it into your own website (good for online learning organizations).

 **Writeboard** (www.writeboard.com): Another stand-alone tool from 37signals, which is integrated into their Basecamp project management system (page 123). Writeboard doesn't allow real-time collaboration, but it's become somewhat of an industry standard.

Real-Time Document Collaboration

A few services out there let you collaborate inside a specific application, such as a spreadsheet or a regular document. Here are a few options:

 **Google Docs** (www.docs.google.com): It doesn't get more real-time than this. Google Docs, an online competitor to Microsoft Office, lets you create spreadsheets, documents, presentations and forms. The cool thing about it is that you can collaborate on your documents with others. While you're working in a shared document, you can see who else is looking at the file with you. If they make a change, you can see them typing or moving things around. It's kind of eerie. See page 146 for a list full of Google's free and low-cost online tools.

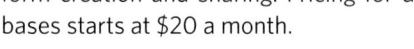 **MyTaskHelper** (mytaskhelper.com): Online database and form creation and sharing. Pricing for unlimited users and data-bases starts at $20 a month.

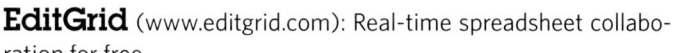 **EditGrid** (www.editgrid.com): Real-time spreadsheet collabo-ration for free.

 **LucidChart** (www.lucidchart.com): Flowchart maker with a very simple interface and easy construction. I'm not sure when you might need to do real-time collaboration to make a flowchart, but this allows it, complete with group chat.

20
Fax and Phone Tools

Will the fax machine ever die?

Even though we e-mail, text, IM, tweet and Skype our way through most days, we can't seem to completely get rid of the need to fax things. This chapter shares several free tools that allow you to both send and receive faxes without actually having a fax machine.

In addition, this chapter includes services from a trend that appeared in the last five years or so: free conference calling, which allows participants to dial a regular phone number (not toll free) into a conference line. Each participant simply dials the number and pays any regular long-distance charges, which are usually minimal since most of us how have low-cost or flat-rate pricing.

Another trend in communications is making phone calls via the Internet. This section also includes tools and services for low-cost online calls.

IN THIS CHAPTER:

eFax Free

www.efax.com/efax-free

 GET YOUR (FREE) FAX RIGHT HERE!

eFax will provide you with a free phone number so you can receive faxes electronically. Just give the number out as you would a real fax number, and the faxes you receive will come to you via e-mail as an attachment. You have to download their software to be able to read the attachment, of course, but it's a small price to pay if you don't want to buy an actual fax machine (or figure out how to hook up your all-in-one, which has been sitting in a box in your garage for two years.)

Note – you cannot send faxes with eFax Free. eFax Plus starts at $14.13 a month if you pay for a year. When you get the Plus edition, you can get a fax number with your area code and send faxes through e-mail.

198

FaxZero

www.faxzero.com

FREE
With ads, or $1.99 without.

 FREE INTERNET FAXING

I was so happy when I discovered FaxZero. What a cool thing. You upload a document or PDF to fax to anyone for free (maximum three pages, two free faxes a day). The cover page will contain an ad – not a problem for most faxes I need to send. But if I need something more professional, I can pay $1.99 and fax up to 15 pages with an ad-free cover sheet.

With FaxZero, you can send a fax for free to any fax machine in the US or Canada, or internationally for a small one-time charge.

☑ **PRIVACY CHECK:** The full privacy policy is available on the host company's site, but the FAQs state, "We hate junk e-mail and junk faxes, and will absolutely not send any unsolicited e-mail or faxes." You can sign up for the mailing list for updates that may include ads. Further, "Your name, company name, e-mail address and fax number will appear in the 'Sender Information' area of the faxes that you send. FaxZero will not share your information, nor information about the people you send faxes to, with marketers or anyone else, unless compelled to do so by court order."

199

ALSO CHECK OUT

 **GotFreeFax.com** (www.gotfreefax.com): No ads, even on the free version, and you can send a rich text document. Up to two free faxes per day of up to three pages each.

 **FaxOrama** (www.faxorama.com): Another free outgoing fax service. Up to two faxes a day, five pages per fax.

Google Voice

www.google.com/voice

 NOT A PHONE LINE, BUT DEFINITELY A PHONE SERVICE

Google Voice is a Google toy, and I'm excited to play with it. If you use Google Voice with your existing phone number, the system will transcribe your voicemail messages and send them to you via text or e-mail. You'll also be able to search the text of the voicemails. It's not exactly a phone service, but you can initiate calls from within the application, and your phone will ring to establish a connection between you and your contact.

If you sign up to get a number from Google Voice, you can program your phones to ring when that number is called – all your other phones, or just the one you choose.

Says one of my readers, "It's the only number I give anyone. Great service that's a huge benefit to telecommuters and travelers. Instead of asking clients or colleagues to call a few different phone number to find you, Google Voice takes care of it."

Vonage
www.vonage.com

Price
Basic plan is $25.99 a month.

 VOICE OVER INTERNET PROTOCOL (VOIP) PHONE LINE

When Internet phone lines first came out, we were all pretty skeptical of this whole "voice over Internet protocol" business. About six years ago my former company wanted to save a few bucks and converted the whole office phone system to VoIP, and it was a complete disaster: dropped calls, garbled sound, frustrated customers. We switched back in a hurry.

But today, VoIP can be a high-quality communication tool that can save money, provide new venues to communicate and make your phone numbers more portable. When I moved into my new office (the one with the view of the Pacific Ocean and easy access to cupcake joints – could I be much happier?), AT&T said they wouldn't let me keep my landline phone number, so I took a deep breath and switched to Vonage, taking my number with me.

I was afraid I'd see a decrease in quality, but except for a few little snarls every once in a while, it sounds just like a landline. I decreased my monthly phone bill, and I increased the portability of the number as well as the features. For example, when I get a voicemail, Vonage transcribes it for me and sends it via e-mail. Pretty cool.

They have more expensive and less expensive packages. Includes unlimited calling to 60+ countries.

201

ALSO CHECK OUT

 **magicJack** (www.magicjack.com): I was insanely skeptical about this service, which allows you to plug a device into your computer (with high-speed Internet) and make as many calls as you want on a regular phone for 20 bucks a year. But one of my friends has it, and he says it's just like a regular phone. The device costs $39.95 and includes the first year's service.

PC Magazine gives magicJack mixed reviews for both customer service and quality of calls. Another big drawback is that your computer has to be on and not in a hibernation mode for magic-Jack to work, otherwise the calls go to voicemail.

Skype
www.skype.com

TALK FOR FREE ONLINE AND CHEAPLY VIA PHONE

In the world of online calling and VoIP, Skype is royalty. The name came from a mash of "sky" and "peer-to-peer conversations." Skype is a free download that allows you to chat via text or talk directly to another Skype viewer using a microphone and/or webcam.

Skype also allows people to quickly share files and collaborate. Many businesses (including my former company) conduct regular meetings via Skype, or just use it to pop off quick questions to colleagues across the hall.

In addition to the communication to other Skype users, Skype allows you to make low-cost calls to landlines and mobiles. The company told me, "Skype is not a replacement for your traditional telephone service and cannot be used for emergency calling," but I know many people who rely on it for their main phone line. And I love news shows and celebrities like Oprah Winfrey use Skype to interview people remotely.

In addition to the basic functionality of Skype, you'll find a kabillion integrations with all sorts of free and low-cost tools to increase productivity, enhance communication and generally make you a more efficient professional, student or regular old computer user.

When I asked Ann Handley, chief content officer of MarketingProfs (www.marketingprofs.com), for her favorite free tools, Skype was at the top of the list:

Skype is software application that allows its user to make voice calls over the Internet. It also allows users to IM and send files. This is a great tool for virtual companies like mine because it connects all of us in a kind of "network." We can also shoot files back and forth, or share links, or discuss things in group chats. I can talk to contributors and co-workers around the world. Did I mention it's totally free?

203
—

SMARTPHONE APPS:

➡ BlackBerry

➡ iPhone

➡ Android

➡ HTC

Readers love it:

"Skype has a fair amount of worldwide accessibility, making it a great way to connect with people you did not converse with as easily before online tools like Skype existed."

Bonnie Koenig, international development and strategic thinking consultant for Going International, www.goinginternational.com

"Free international calls! I use it for consulting, interviews and calling home while at conferences."

Chris Garrett, new media consultant and co-author of ProBlogger: Secrets for Blogging Your Way to a Six-Figure Income, *www.chrisg.com*

"It's free, and an easy way to communicate with friends and family. After downloading and installing Skype, all you have to do is add other users to your contact list, and click the call button!"

Courtney Moltzen, cognitive science major at the University of California, San Diego

"As a telecommuter, Skype keeps me connected with my co-workers. We use it every day to ask quick questions of each other and just to touch base. You can find out an answers to something in about 10 seconds as opposed to having to wait for an e-mail to go through."

Meg Tully, nonprofit consultant for Nonprofit Know How, www.npfknowhow.com

ALSO CHECK OUT

 **Logitech Vid** (sn.im/logitech_vid): Webcam maker Logitech created a free, easy-to-use video call program to let people use their new webcams. It's a little hard to find on their site, so I created a shortened URL to the download site.

 **ooVoo** (www.oovoo.com): High-definition video conferencing for up to six, plus desktop sharing capabilities. Free for 3-way calls with no desktop sharing. More capabilities and 5-way video calls start at $9.95 a month.

Yahoo, Google and several other providers also integrate voice and video into their instant message chats.

Free Teleconferencing

In addition to new less expensive telephone communication options, a number of services these days offer free phone conferencing. Phone conference lines used to cost quite a bit. You had to have a 1-800 number for everyone to call, and it would cost the host several cents per minute per participant.

But these days you can find quite a few free conference call companies that provide you a run-of-the-mill phone number (not toll free) and a pass code, and all your participants dial the number to get into the call. Each participant has to pay regular long-distance charges for the call, but many of us have unlimited calling plans, so the call doesn't really cost us anything. And most companies will also record your calls for free, so these services are great when you're doing a training session.

Here are a few of my favorites:

 **FreeConferenceCall.com** (www.freeconferencecall.com)

 **Powwownow** (www.powwownow.com)

InstantConference (www.instantconference.com)

21

Tools to Share Information

Isn't it only fair to share?

This chapter should really be called, "HEY – It's Right Here!" because these tools allow you to send and share information with your teammates. Rather than sending an entire Web page and hoping your recipient will figure out the exact point you want to make, some of these tools, such as the Awesome Highlighter (page 211), allow you to select specific text to share.

This chapter also includes a long list of URL shorteners, which are wonderful for sharing links to Web pages on Twitter, Facebook and more. Plus, this chapter includes tools to share large files, which is an essential when working with groups.

IN THIS CHAPTER:

Long URL Shrinkers

Because of horrible, malicious virus writers who spend their days trying to figure out clever ways to take over our computers, our bank accounts and the universe, we are warned again and again to never click on anything that we don't recognize. I used to tell students in my computer courses, "Even if your grandmother sends you a link, be suspicious. Make sure you know where you're going before you click."

This is great advice, or it was until a couple of years ago, when Twitter's 140-character limits meant that we would be 11 characters over just by pasting a link such as www.AskBethZ.com/2010/03/PDFescape-the-PDF-editor-ive-been-dreaming-ofe-online-PDF-reader-editor-form-filler-form-designer-solution/.

With Twitter and other services, brevity is imperative. So they started creating URL shortening services that let you convert a long URL into a teeny, tiny one.

Now back to the security issue. If your grandmother sends you a long link like the one above, you'd probably trust it. But what if the link she sends is z.pe/56IG? You may think your grandmother has become a hacker.

Some people have an inherent (and justified) fear of shortened URLs since you can't see what you're clicking on. But I have good news. A 2010 study by Zscaler Inc., a company that sells security services, looked for malicious content in 1.3 million shortened links taken from Twitter over two weeks. Just 773 of those links – 0.06 percent – were malicious. The rest were just grandmothers and regular users like you and me sharing information and resources with others.

Here are just a few URL shorteners that I use:

 **Goo.gl** (goo.gl): Brought to us by the mighty Google folks, a simple shortener with stats.

 **bit.ly** (bit.ly): Twitter's shortener of choice.

 **BudURL** (budurl.com): It's a long link, but BudURL offers all kinds of tracking information to help with your marketing.

 **Is.gd** (is.gd): I love this little guy. It has no bells or whistles, but it stands for "is good." That makes me happy.

 **Threely** (3.ly): Lets your viewers preview the link before they click and allows custom URLs, such as 3.ly/AskBethZ (goes to www.AskBethZ.com, of course).

  **TinyURL** (tinyurl.com): The first service I discovered that would shrink a long link into a short one. They're still around, but now the URL seems impossibly long.

 **URL Sniffer** (urlsniffer.info): Drag the URL Sniffer bookmarklet to your Web browser to convert shortened URLs to their original and pre-test the link.

CHEAP CASE STUDY	**Using URL shorteners to track popular content**
	Ann Handley

Bit.ly allows users to shorten, share and track links (URLs). Reducing the URL length, of course, makes sharing easier. I share links that MarketingProfs publishes frequently via e-mail/my blog/social media sites like Twitter and Facebook. When I use bit.ly to shorten the link, I get a robust read of what's popular and what's not; it's like a mini and instant Google Analytics (page 117)!

Ann Handley, chief content officer, MarketingProfs (www.marketingprofs.com)

Awesome Highlighter www.awesomehighlighter.com	**FREE**

 HIGHLIGHT INFORMATION ON THE WEB

The Awesome Highlighter is just that ... awesome! Go to their site and enter the URL of a page with information you want to share. The Awesome Highlighter then takes you to your page and turns your curser into a little highlighter. Select the text you want to share, add a note, then click done. You'll get a link to a page with just that highlighted information that you can easily share.

If you register, you can organize your own highlights and use the service to create a little library of resources you've discovered. It works in most browsers, and you can download a plug-in for Firefox to capture things without having to go to their site.

JUST 'CUZ YOU CAN

 Ever need to dash off a quick text to someone while you're at your desk? You have to get up, hunt down your phone, press all those dang buttons ... Wouldn't it be easier if you could just do it from your computer?

Ta dah! Joopz can help. **Joopz** (www.joopz.com) lets you send and receive text messages from your computer. You can create groups of up to 10 people, so you can text several at once. You can schedule reminders and program it to send texts at a certain time. Cool stuff. The free version gives you 50 outgoing messages a month. For or $2.95 a month a year or $2.95 a month, the unlimited version has plug-ins for your desktop and Outlook.

Streamfile

www.streamfile.com

FREE

For the basics, but files larger than 150MB need the Pro version.

 SEND A LARGE FILE FOR FREE

Streamfile is not the only free file transfer webware out there, but it's one of the easiest. Simply put in someone's e-mail address and upload your file. Accept the terms and hit send. The file (up to 150MB for the free version, up to 30GB for the paid) stays up for 24 hours.

Easy, easy. I sent myself a 7MB file in 30 seconds. The same file took at least 90 seconds when it cleared my Outlook outbox the other day. Cons: Use the advanced options to add your name to the e-mail or it comes from the Streamfile Team and will go straight into a spam filter.

Another cool feature: When you send a file with Streamfile, your recipient can can start downloading before the upload is completed.

ALSO CHECK OUT

 **DropSend** (www.dropsend.com): Send up to 2GB up to five times a month for free. Next level starts at $5 a month.

 **YouSendIt** (www.yousendit.com): Longstanding favorite in this category. Free up to 100MB, and other levels start at $9.99. YouSendIt has plug-ins that integrate with many desktop applications, including Outlook, Office, Photoshop and more. Plus it'll work on an iPhone or BlackBerry.

JUST 'CUZ YOU CAN

 How many of your friends and distant cousins forward you their angel wishes, pleas to help a fictitious missing girl or warnings of kidney-stealing prostitutes? Use **StopForwarding.com** (www.stopforwarding.com) to politely and anonymously ask them to stop forwarding you junk e-mail.

Your friend will receive this from the site:

Hi Steve,

One of your friends has sent you this message from StopForwarding.Com, the website that allows individuals to politely and anonymously e-mail their friends and ask that they stop the habit of sending forwarded e-mails or FWDs.

Please do not forward chain letters, urban legends, potentially offensive jokes, videos or photos without being asked or first receiving permission. If you find something that you want to pass on and you genuinely think the recipient will enjoy it then forward it to that person only (not in an e-mail blast to all your friends and family) and include a personal note about why you enjoyed it and why you think they will too. Avoid sending forwards to friends or relatives that you've grown distant with. It can be frustrating for the recipient when the only correspondence he or she has with someone is via impersonal, unwanted e-mail.

For more tips on e-mail etiquette, visit www.StopForwarding.Com

Thank you,

A Friend (via www.StopForwarding.Com)

22
Social Media Tools

You do know *The Social Network* wasn't fiction, right?

I asked several best-selling authors to share their favorite free and low-cost tools, and most of them came back with recommendations for social networking tools. This chapter contains a few social media tools that of my favorite experts consider essential.

I threw my pick in among the experts' because StumbleUpon (page 217) is my favorite tool to discover free and low-cost tools. Visit my page to see what I've bookmarked: www.stumbleupon.com/stumbler/avenuez.

IN THIS CHAPTER:

Layar

layar.com

FREE

 FIND ANYTHING, ANYWHERE WITH YOUR IPHONE

This book doesn't really cover iPhone applications, but some of them are just too good to resist, especially when bestselling author David Meerman Scott tells me that it's his favorite free tool. Scott, author of *The New Rules of Marketing & PR*, now published in 24 languages, says "I love the free Layar application on my iPhone because no matter where I am in the world, I can quickly find the perfect place to eat, drink or hang out."

As soon as he told me about it, I downloaded it myself, and I have to agree: Layar is awesome. Download this free little app onto your iPhone, and see what you've been missing in your backyard. The phone picks up your location, and you apply a filter (layer) to see what's happening around you. For example, you can overlay the map of your area with a layer showing the people on Twitter who are tweeting near you. You can also search the Yellow Pages layer for "cupcake" to find the nearest cupcake hubs.

The site calls this view of the world "Augmented Reality," as in, "We augment the real world as seen through your mobile phone, based on your location."

SMARTPHONE APPS: iPhone and Android

Squidoo

www.squidoo.com

VIEW YOUR INTERESTS THROUGH
AN ONLINE LENS YOU CREATE

When I wrote to THE Seth Godin, bestselling author and one of the world's foremost marketing gurus, he wrote me back almost immediately with his favorite free tool:

"I'm the founder of squidoo.com, and we started it four years to raise money for charity and to be in this book. It's a free service that PAYS YOU or your favorite charity to promote yourself, your books or your business. Really."

I'm always a sucker for charitable causes, and Squidoo makes it easy to be a fan. You set up your own site about something that interests you – as Seth said, it could be your hobbies, your books or your business. Then you start collecting and creating information on your topic. You establish lenses, which are pages, similar to flyers or overviews, that gather everything you have gathered about your topic.

Like the lens of a camera, you snap all the disparate information into focus. Your Squidoo is your perspective on something, and it's your chance to showcase what you've discovered and what you know.

The site accepts advertising, and if your lens is popular and people click on ads while they're visiting, you receive half of the advertising revenue. The company uses 45 percent of the ad revenue to keep running, and the remaining 5 percent goes to charity.

StumbleUpon

www.stumbleupon.com

FREE

 DISCOVER NEW SITES

StumbleUpon takes you to sites and resources you never knew existed. I set it up for my husband, who likes jazz and cycling, and he discovered radio stations he had never heard of that play classic jazz on the Web.

When you sign up, you can install a toolbar into your browser. Hit the Stumble button to get started with your Web discoveries. If you're more interested in running than in raquetball today, you can fine tune the Stumble recommendations in the toolbar.

When you find something you like, hit the Thumbs Up button on the toolbar. StumbleUpon saves it for you and remembers that you like those types of sites. If you don't like a site, there's a Thumbs Down button so Stumble knows not to bring you to similar sites again.

I can't tell you how many cool things I've discovered here, including many of the free and low-cost tools in this book.

CHEAP TIP

StumbleUpon has a cool advertising option, Paid Discovery, that lets you pay a nickel per hit for traffic to your site. If your visitors like your site and give a couple of Thumbs Up, StumbleUpon will start sending nonpaid traffic there, and you could get way more hits than you paid for.

SMARTPHONE APP: iPhone

CHEAP CASE STUDY	**My Favorite Tools**
	Jessica Smith (@JessicaKnows)

 **Picnik** (page 54): I can change the look of my blog header in a snap with this easy photo editing on the web.

 **Tumblr** (www.tumblr.com) Think Tumblr's just a free blogging platform? I also track my press and blog mentions and embed on my own blog as a "Recent Press" page.

 **Google Alerts** (page 105): lets me keep tracking what people are saying about me so I can respond (or not) as needed.

 **Hootsuite** (page 219): is unlike other Twitter tools. It's Web based so I don't get timed out from volume of tweets from the 21k+ people I'm following.

Social media goddess Jessica Smith, aka @JessicaKnows on Twitter, is a vice president in Fleishman-Hillard's Digital practice group. She first got online in junior high when her dad hooked her up with a Prodigy account. Visit her website at www.JessicaKnows.com.

Twitter

www.Twitter.com

FREE

 **MICROBLOGGING AND SOCIAL NETWORKING**

It's time, my friends. You need to get involved with social media to grow your business. Bestselling author Chris Brogan (www.chrisbrogan.com) told me Twitter was one of his top three essential tools.

Twitter brings together millions of users who write brief (I mean really brief) updates, answers to the simple question: What's happening?

Twitter takes some getting used to. The first few tweets you receive may say things like, "I just ate a bologna sandwich," and "I really need to pee, but I'm stuck in this meeting." But after a while, you'll catch on. You need to give to get back. People share breaking news, business-building tips, helpful blog resources and new friends and contacts. It's really a fantastic way to grow your network, enhance your brand and meet wonderful people.

Start by following me at www.Twitter.com/AskBethZ (or my publisher at www.Twitter.com/TSTCPublishing)!

ALSO CHECK OUT

 **Hootsuite** (www.hootsuite.com): At last count, I think there were a billion different Twitter applications to help you manage the tool. Ok, maybe only half a billion. But one of the tools that several readers recommended for business use was Hootsuite. Hootsuite merges all your Twitter accounts into one dashboard. It allows you to schedule tweets, personalize your dashboard, combine other social networks and bring your professional teammates together. There's an iPhone app as well. Free.

About Your Nerdy Best Friend

BETH ZIESENIS

Beth Ziesenis is an author, speaker, marketing analyst and complete tech geek. Since her first Commodore 64 computer, she has been fascinated with technology and computer shortcuts that make people's lives easier. From her home base in sunny San Diego, California, Beth helps computer users all over the country filter through thousands of apps, gadgets, widgets and doodads to find the perfect free and bargain technology tools for business and personal use. She loves to keep up with all the new online applications and downloads that can help you look like you're working with a team of marketing, computer and productivity experts, even if you suffer from a shrinking staff and a disappearing budget. Beth shares these tools online at AskBethZ (www.AskBethZ.com) and in person at presentations. And she's even been known to pass on a few tips over cupcakes and coffee.

Want to contact Beth? Drop her a line at beth@askbethz.com.
Or, just scan this QR code:

TSTC Publishing

Established in 2004, TSTC Publishing is a provider of high-end technical instructional materials and related information to institutions of higher education and private industry. "High end" refers simultaneously to the information delivered, the various delivery formats of that information, and the marketing of materials produced. More information about the products and services offered by TSTC Publishing may be found at its website: publishing.tstc.edu.